Stormy Skies, Valiant Souls

The USAAF 3rd Bombardment Division in World War II
Daniel L. Couzens

Castle Vale Publishers Ltd

Contents

Copyright	V
Dedication	VI
Introduction Setting the Stage	1
Chapter 1 The Aerodromes of the 3rd Air Division 1943-1945	6
Chapter 2 The 4th Combat Bombardment Wing	10
Chapter 3 The 13th Combat Bombardment Wing	26
Chapter 4 The 45th Combat Bombardment Wing	44
Chapter 5 The 93rd Combat Bombardment Wing	57
Chapter 6 The Bomber Aircraft of the 3rd Air Division	70

Chapter 7 The VIII Fighter Command	92
Chapter 8 The Fighter Aircraft of the 66th Fighter Wing	96
Chapter 9 Valor in the Skies: The 3rd Air Division's Standout Bombing Missions	126
Chapter 10 Guardians of the Skies: The 3rd Air Division's Aces	153
Conclusion Reflection and Impact	182
About the Author	186
Picture Credits	188

Copyright © 2024 by Daniel L Couzens

All rights reserved.

The content contained within this book may not be reproduced, duplicated or transmitted without direct written permission from the author or the publisher. Under no circumstances will any blame or legal responsibility be held against the publisher, or author, for any damages, reparation, or monetary loss due to the information contained within this book, either directly or indirectly.

Legal Notice: This book is copyright protected. It is only for personal use. You cannot amend, distribute, sell, use, quote or paraphrase any part, or the content within this book, without the consent of the author or publisher.

Disclaimer Notice: Please note the information contained within this document is for educational and entertainment purposes only. All effort has been executed to present accurate, up to date, reliable, complete information. No warranties of any kind are declared or implied. The content within this book has been derived from various sources. By reading this document, the reader agrees that under no circumstances is the author responsible for any losses, direct or indirect, that are incurred as a result of the use of the information contained within this document, including, but not limited to, errors, omissions, or inaccuracies

Dedication

This book is dedicated to:

The men and women of the US Eighth Air Force, particularly those of the 3rd Bombardment Division, who fought courageously in a faraway land so they may ensure peace and freedom in their own country, free from the tyranny of Nazism.

Further I must thank my wife for her courage, fortitude and resilience in starting her own book publishing company and allowing me the latitude to publish works under her firm - thank you, Kiks!

Lastly, I thank the teams at Chat GPT and GAB AI for helping me research this book as a commemoration to the brave airmen and women of the Eighth Air Force in Europe. What I have learnt is that AI is not to be feared, and instead used as a tool to help humanity achieve greatness. As a 'Forbes 500' AI firm-owning CEO recently told me, "How can AI compete with humanity when we can't understand our own consciousness, let alone define it? True AI is at least 100 years in the future."

Introduction
Setting the Stage

The personnel of the United States Army Air Force (USAAF) stationed in East Anglia, England, during World War II were truly remarkable. Their bravery and dedication to their mission were unparalleled, and they played a pivotal role in the war effort. This book is a tribute to their sacrifices and the impact they had on history, so that we might enjoy our freedoms today.

The USAAF units were tasked with bombing Nazi Germany by day, while the British Royal Air Force (RAF) conducted bombing missions by night. Daylight bombing was a dangerous and demanding task, but these brave men took on the challenge with determination and courage. They flew over hostile territory, facing enemy fire and harsh weather conditions, all in the name of protecting the allied forces and defeating the enemy. Their unwavering commitment to their mission and each other is a testament to the strength of the human spirit. Through the pages of this book, we will delve into the stories of these brave airmen, their triumphs and their struggles, their victories and their losses. We will honor their legacy and ensure their sacrifices are never forgotten. This is a story of courage, resilience, and sacrifice – a story that deserves to be told and remembered for generations to come. Let us pay homage to these heroes of the USAAF and their crucial role in the fight against Nazi-led tyranny.

The Eighth Air Force played a vital role in the Allied air campaign during World War II. Stationed across East Anglia, England, this unit was responsible for conducting strategic bombing missions against Germany and occupied Europe during daylight hours. The Eighth Air Force was broken down into three main bombardment divisions: the 1st, 2nd, and 3rd, and were supported by the VIII Fighter Wing. The 3rd Bombardment Division consisted of the following bombardment wings with each made up of around three to four bombardment groups:

- 4th Combat Bombardment Wing, callsign

Frankilin/Hotshot

- 13th Combat Bombardment Wing, callsign Zootsuit/Fireball

- 45th Combat Bombardment Wing, callsign Wolfgang/Vampire

- 93rd Combat Bombardment Wing, callsign Clambake

By mid-1944, the Eighth Air Force had reached a total strength of more than 200,000 personnel (it is estimated that more than 350,000 Americans served in the Eighth Air Force during the war in Europe.) At peak strength, the Eighth Air Force had forty heavy bomber groups, fifteen fighter groups, and four specialized support groups.

On February 22, 1944, the United States Strategic and Tactical Air Forces (USSTAF) of Europe were established, and the Eighth Air Force absorbed the VIII Bomber Command, VIII Fighter Command, and VIII Air Support Command under a single headquarters. The organization of bomber and fighter resources was now under the 1st, 2nd, and 3rd Air Divisions rather than Bombardment Divisions.

The focus of this book is the 3rd Air Division (AD), (prior to April 1944, the 3rd Bombardment Division) its bases, aircraft, and airmen. One of the 3rd AD's most famous units, the 100th Bomb Group, has now been immortalized in the new Apple TV drama 'Masters of the Air', directed by Tom Hanks and Steven Spielberg from the book of the same name, by Donald L. Miller.

Overall, the airfields and units of the Eighth Air Force in East Anglia played a vital role in the Allied effort to defeat Germany during World War II. They conducted numerous bombing missions and provided essential support to the ground forces, contributing significantly to the eventual Allied victory.

Not to diminish the legacy of the 1st and 2nd ADs that were also part of the Eight Air Force, this book will concentrate on the 3rd AD. To cover all the airfields, units, and men of the Eighth Air Force, it would require at least another two books! The men of the 3rd AD were a diverse group, hailing from all corners of the United States. They were brought together by a common goal: to defeat the enemy and bring peace to the world.

These brave airmen left behind their families and loved ones to serve their country, and their sacrifices would not go unnoticed. Day after day, they flew over enemy territory, facing constant danger and uncertainty. The roar of the engines and the sound of gunfire were their constant companions. But through it all, they remained steadfast and resolute, knowing that their mission was critical to the success of the Allies.

They became 'masters of the air', navigating through treacherous skies and delivering their payloads with precision and accuracy. Their tales stand as evidence of their fortitude and the strong bonds between comrades. They faced insurmountable odds, but through their courage and determination, they emerged victorious. The legacy of the 3rd AD will continue to inspire future generations, reminding us of the true cost of freedom and the bravery of those who fought for it.

Chapter 1
The Aerodromes of the 3rd Air Division 1943-1945

In the annals of World War II history, the role of air power, especially that of the US Eighth Air Force, stands as evidence to the strategic shift towards aerial dominance in military doctrine. Nestled within the broader narrative of the air war over Europe, the 3rd AD played a pivotal role in executing precision daylight bombing missions that targeted the Nazi war machine's heart. The stage for these monumental efforts was set in the rolling countryside of eastern England, where a network of aerodromes became the launchpad for operations that would significantly impact the war's outcome.

The next few chapters will introduce the reader to the aerodromes that served as the backbone for the 3rd AD's operations. These bases, scattered across the East Anglian landscape, were not merely geographical locations but epicenters of courage, innovation, and relentless pursuit of victory against a formidable adversary. Each aerodrome, with its runways, grass strips, hangars, and control towers, was a microcosm of the broader war effort, teeming with the lives of pilots, crew members, engineers, and support staff, all unified in their mission to secure freedom from tyranny. My grandfather was a foreman for Walter E. Lawrence Ltd. during the war and was involved in the construction of many East Anglian aerodromes, as he used to call them. He helped with the construction of RAF Watton, RAF Bircham Newton, RAF East Wretham, and RAF Bodney, to name a few – many of which were later homes to famous USAAF units.

The establishment of these aerodromes was a feat of engineering and logistical planning. Amidst the uncertainty of war and the constant threat of enemy action, the construction and operation of these bases demonstrated the Allies' resolve and adaptability. From the rustic charm of rural England, these aerodromes transformed into bustling hubs of military activity, where B-17 Flying Fortresses and

B-24 Liberators (among other aircraft) were readied for their perilous journeys into occupied Europe.

As we delve into the stories of these aerodromes, we explore not only the strategic significance of each location but also the human element that infused these bases with life. The narrative intertwines tales of bravery in the skies with the daily grind on the ground, where maintenance crews worked tirelessly to ensure each aircraft was battle-ready. It is a story of technological innovation, as strategies and equipment evolved in response to the challenges posed by the enemy and the demanding nature of the missions.

The following chapters highlight how these aerodromes served as vital links in the chain of Allied air strategy. Positioned strategically across Eastern England, they enabled the 3rd AD to participate in critical bombing campaigns such as the destruction of the German Luftwaffe during the Big Week, the crippling of the Nazi oil industry, and the preparation for the D-Day landings through the targeting of German fortifications along the French coast.

In recounting the history of these aerodromes, we pay homage to the legacy of those who served within the 3rd AD. Their contributions, made from the runways and grass strips of England, were instrumental in shaping the course of World War II. This chapter invites readers to embark on a journey through time, to walk the runways of the past, and to remember the valor and sacrifice that defined the air war over Europe.

Chapter 2
The 4th Combat Bombardment Wing

RAF Rougham

RAF Rougham (also known as RAF Bury St. Edmunds), nestled in the Suffolk countryside near Bury St. Edmunds, England, holds a significant place in the history of World War II. Initially constructed by the RAF in 1941, the airfield evolved into an important base for the USAAF as they launched daylight bombing raids over Nazi-occupied Europe. In 1942, the RAF handed over Rougham to the USAAF, redesignating it as Station 468. This transition marked the beginning of a pivotal chapter in the airfield's history, as it became home to several USAAF units tasked with conducting strategic bombing missions.

The 322nd Bombardment Group (BG) was among the first USAAF units to arrive at RAF Rougham in December 1942. Operating B-26 Marauder medium bombers, this group quickly became involved in a relentless campaign against Axis targets. Their missions took them deep into enemy territory, striking key installations and transportation networks, significantly contributing to the war effort.

Early in 1943, the 94th BG (Heavy) took up residence at RAF Rougham. Their tail marking was a black square (like all 3rd AD bomber groups) with a white letter 'A'. Equipped with B-17 Flying Fortress heavy bombers, the 94th BG became a cornerstone of the Eight Air Force's strategic bombing campaign. Their missions, often deep into heavily defended airspace, targeted factories, airfields, and other critical infrastructure. However, the price of their bravery and determination was high.

One fateful day that etched itself into the history books was October 14, 1943. On this tragic date, the 94th BG participated in a mission to strike Schweinfurt, Germany's ball-bearing factories, a vital component of the Nazi war machine. This mission, known as "Black Thursday," proved devastating. German fighters and anti-aircraft fire wrought havoc on the USAAF formations. The 94th BG suffered grievous losses, with numerous B-17 Flying Fortresses falling victim to the relentless enemy fire. The losses incurred on this day had a profound impact on the unit and highlighted the extreme risks undertaken by Allied aircrews.

The losses suffered by USAAF units based at RAF Rougham were a testament to the courage and sacrifice of the airmen who faced formidable challenges in the skies over Europe. Their dedication and resilience were instrumental in the ultimate Allied victory. The 94th BG flew a total of 324 missions in 8,884 sorties from May 13, 1943 to April 21, 1945, and dropped 18,924 tons of bomb while losing 153 aircraft.

In conclusion, RAF Rougham's transformation from an RAF airfield to a key USAAF base during World War II symbolizes the close collaboration between the British and American forces in the fight against the Axis powers. The units stationed there, particularly the 94th BG and the 55th Fighter Group, made significant contributions to the Allied war effort. However, these contributions came at great cost, as evidenced by the significant single-day losses they endured during critical missions. RAF Rougham's history is a reminder of the valor and determination of those who served there, and the sacrifices made in the pursuit of victory.

1. Major Byron Trent of the 94th Bomb Group with a B-17 Flying Fortress (serial number 44-8158) nicknamed "Bobby Sox". Nose art on the airplane created by Sergeant Jay Cowan, 490th Group

RAF Rattlesden

RAF Rattlesden, located in Suffolk, England, was another battle-winning station of the USAAF during World War II. Activated in 1942, the airfield served as a base for bomber squadrons engaged in the intense air campaign against Nazi Germany. The 447th BG (Heavy) was the primary unit stationed at RAF Rattlesden. This group, part of the Eighth Air Force, operated Boeing B-17 Flying Fortress bombers, iconic aircraft that became synonymous with the USAAF's daylight precision bombing strategy. Their tail code was a black square with a white letter 'K'.

The 447th BG comprised four bomb squadrons: the 708th, 709th, 710th, and 711th. The group's combat missions began in December 1943, and from that point on, the 447th participated in numerous strategic bombing missions, targeting industrial and military installations in Germany and occupied territories. RAF Rattlesden's facilities included hangars, control towers, and other essential structures for the maintenance and operation of the B-17 fleet. Ground crews and support personnel worked diligently to prepare the aircraft for their perilous missions. RAF Rattlesden also played an important role beyond its function as a bomber base, serving as a hub for strategic planning, intelligence activities, and logistical support as well.

The airfield's strategic location allowed the B-17s to conduct long-range bombing raids deep into enemy territory, making it a valuable asset to the Eighth Air Force. Although the 447th BG faced the challenges inherent in daylight bombing raids, with the B-17s flying in tight formations to maximize defensive firepower. The crews encountered fierce resistance from German fighters and intense anti-aircraft fire, but their determination and skill were fundamental to the success of their missions.

One of the notable achievements of the 447th BG was its participation in Operation Argument, also known as "Big Week," in February 1944, which was an intensive bombing campaign targeting German aircraft production facilities. On April 29, 1944 the 447th BG participated in a raid against Berlin however en-route the mission went off-course and was attacked by German fighters; they eventually bombed a target of opportunity at Magdeburg although they tragically lost 11 aircraft during the mission, mostly to enemy fighters. The BG also played a significant role in supporting the D-Day invasion on June 6, 1944, by bombing coastal defenses and transportation infrastructure.

Following the conclusion of hostilities in Europe in May 1945, RAF Rattlesden's wartime operations ceased. The airfield was placed in care and maintenance status before being returned to civilian use.

In summary, RAF Rattlesden stands as a testament to the courage and sacrifice of the USAAF personnel who served there. The airfield played a pivotal role in the Eighth Air Force's strategic bombing campaign, contributing significantly to the eventual Allied victory in World War II. The legacy of RAF Rattlesden and the 447th BG remains an integral part of the history of the air war in Europe during that critical period.

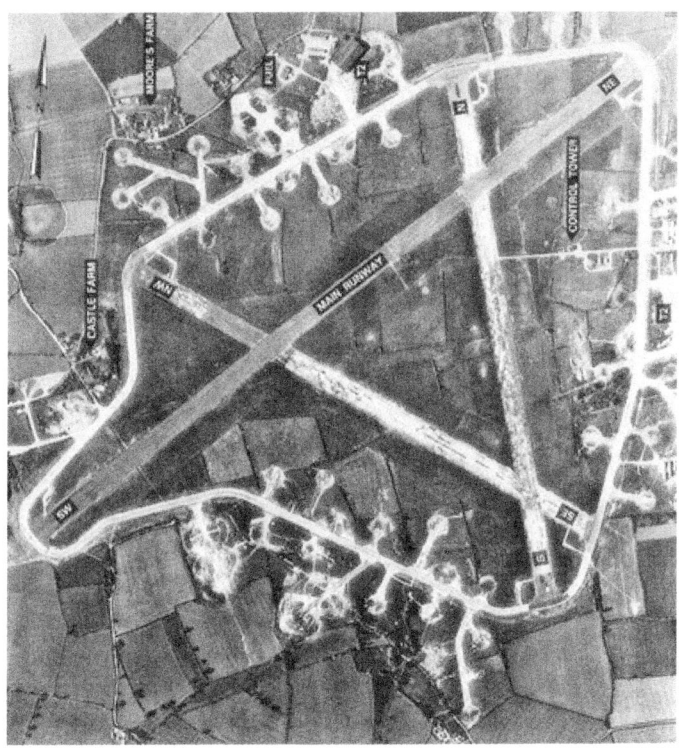

2. Aerial photograph of RAF Rattlesden Airfield, 1946, England

RAF Lavenham

RAF Lavenham, also located in Suffolk, served as a base for the 487th BG, part of the Eighth Air Force's strategic bombing campaign against Nazi Germany. Activated in 1943, RAF Lavenham became operational in 1944 and its strategic location in southeastern England made it an ideal base for long-range bombing missions over occupied Europe and Germany.

The airfield's proximity to the continent allowed American bombers to conduct deep-penetration raids into the heart of enemy territory. The 487th BG, initially equipped with B-24 Liberator bombers, was the primary operational unit stationed at RAF Lavenham, arriving on April 4, 1944. The group consisted of four squadrons: the 837th, 838th, 839th, and 840th Bomb Squadrons. The B-24s were known for their long range and high payload capacity, making them suitable for strategic bombing missions. Their tail marking was a black square with a white letter 'P'.

The first combat mission from RAF Lavenham took place on April 10, 1944, targeting an airfield in Bourges, France. The 487th BG continued to participate in numerous missions throughout the war, focusing on key industrial sites, military installations, and transportation networks in Germany and occupied territories. The aircrew faced formidable challenges during their missions, including encounters with German fighter planes, heavy anti-aircraft fire, and adverse weather conditions. The B-24 Liberators from RAF Lavenham became a familiar sight in the skies over Suffolk as they formed up to head east on their strategic bombing missions. The 487th converted to B-17s on August 1, 1944 and joined the strategic bombing campaigns of the 3rd AD.[1]

On December 24, 1944, the group was the lead on the Eighth Air Force's largest mission of the war. Brigadier General Frederick Castle, commander of the 4th Bombardment Wing, commanded the raid and flew the 487th's lead aircraft. It was his 30th mission. The group was attacked by Luftwaffe interceptors before escorting fighters could join the bomber formation. Three group planes were shot down, and an additional four were abandoned after making emergency landings in Belgium. Among the losses was General Castle's lead plane. He was posthumously awarded the Medal of Honor for taking control of the plane to permit other crew members to bail out and refusing to jettison the plane's bombload to avoid casualties to civilians or friendly troops below. From January 1, 1945 through the end

---

1. Wikipedia

of the war, the group's bombing accuracy was the highest in the 3rd AD.

The 487th BG faced its share of challenges and losses during the war, but it also achieved notable successes. The group earned a Distinguished Unit Citation (DUC) for its outstanding performance during a raid on the synthetic oil refineries at Merseburg, Germany, on November 21, 1944. Despite heavy opposition, the group pressed on to successfully complete its mission, inflicting significant damage on the enemy's industrial capabilities.

Like many airfields in the region, RAF Lavenham faced the constant threat of enemy attacks. While specific incidents of enemy assaults on the airfield may not be as well documented as major events, the overall wartime environment made every airbase susceptible to aerial bombardment.

Following the end of hostilities in Europe in May 1945, RAF Lavenham's wartime role came to an end. The airfield was placed in care and maintenance status before being returned to the RAF in 1948.

3. "A B-26 about to buzz RAF Lavenham". View is to the west and the buildings at left are 839th BS offices. Two B-24's parked across field are said to likely be 42-94756 and 41-29488

RAF Sudbury

During World War II, RAF Sudbury played a weighty role in the operations of the USAAF European operations. The airfield was initially built by the RAF in 1943 as a satellite airfield for RAF Stradishall. However, in early 1944, it was handed over to the USAAF and renamed as Station 174. The first USAAF unit to be stationed at Sudbury was the 486th BG, equipped with B-24 Liberator bombers. The 486th BG arrived at Sudbury in April 1944 and began conducting bombing missions over occupied Europe soon after. They were joined by other USAAF units, such as the 527th Air Service Group, which provided support services for the operations at Sudbury. Their tail marking was a black square with the white letter 'W'.

The main mission of the USAAF at RAF Sudbury was to conduct strategic bombing raids against industrial and military targets in Germany. These missions were carried out by the B-24 Liberator bombers, which had a long range and were capable of carrying a significant number of bombs. One of the most notable operations conducted by the USAAF at Sudbury was the bombing of the Nazi-controlled V-1 rocket sites in northern France. These sites were responsible for launching the V-1 flying bombs, also known as "buzz bombs", which were causing significant damage and casualties in England.

In addition to conducting bombing missions, the USAAF at Sudbury also played an important role in the transportation of supplies and personnel. The airfield was used as a transit point for aircraft and personnel heading to other bases in Europe, as well as for receiving supplies and reinforcements. The

USAAF units at RAF Sudbury also had a significant impact on the local community. The airfield was surrounded by small villages, and the American airmen stationed there often interacted with the locals, bringing a taste of American culture to the English countryside. The airmen also participated in various community events, such as sports tournaments and dances, further strengthening the bond between the two nations.

Unfortunately, the operations at RAF Sudbury and local stations were not without casualties. The USAAF lost numerous aircraft and crew members during bombing missions, and the local area also experienced some damage from stray bombs. An aircraft crash occurred not far from RAF Sudbury near Long Melford on May 20, 1944. A B-24 Liberator from the 487th Bomb Group from RAF Lavenham crashed in woodland near Kentwell Hall after its number two engine failed shortly after takeoff. The aircraft burst into flames upon impact. Rescue efforts were led by Police Sergeant Ronald Saunders, who, along with others, helped save crew members from the burning wreckage. Six crew members died in the crash, while others sustained life-changing injuries but survived.

A grim tale of the murder of seven airmen from the 486th whose B-17 (43-37909) crashed near Borkum Island, Germany, on August 4, 1944 has been documented too. The B-17 collided with another B-17, and confusion reigned as two of the crew members (Sgt Rachak and 2nd Lt L Ingerson) bailed out after they mistakenly thought they heard the bailout bell. The remaining seven crew members stayed on board, and the pilot, 2nd Lt. Walthall, managed to recover the plane and land it on a beach. The remaining seven crew members were captured and marched through the town, where they were physically abused by the locals. The march ended with the airmen being murdered—shot in the head by a German soldier. After the war, charges were brought against twenty-three civilians and military personnel for the murders, but only fifteen were arrested. The crew were originally buried at Borkum Cemetery, graves D4 to D10, but were repatriated some years later.

The USAAF continued its operations at RAF Sudbury until the end of the war in Europe in May 1945. After the war, the airfield was briefly used by the RAF before being abandoned in 1946. Today, the site of the former airfield is mostly used for agriculture, with few remnants of the airfield remaining. Though the airfield is no longer in use, it remains an important part of the history of the USAAF and their contributions to the Allied victory in Europe.

4. Former RAF Sudbury from the air in 2011

Chapter 3
The 13th Combat Bombardment Wing

RAF Horham

RAF Horham, located in of Suffolk, was originally built in the late 1930s as a satellite airfield for RAF Eye, another nearby base. However, as tensions rose in Europe and the threat of war loomed, the British government decided to expand the airfield at Horham to accommodate the growing needs of the RAF.

In 1942, the airfield was transferred to the USAAF as part of the lease agreement between the United States and the United Kingdom. The USAAF immediately began extensive renovations and construction at RAF Horham to turn it into a fully operational base. The main runway was lengthened and reinforced to accommodate the larger American bombers, and several new buildings, including hangars, barracks, and administrative offices, were built. The base also had its own water and sewage treatment plants, as well as a power station, to support the large number of personnel stationed there. Initially home to the 47th BG, the unit subsequently became part of the Twelfth Air Force, and in January 1943, the 323nd BG became resident with the B-26 Marauder. Some six months later, the 323nd BG transferred to Earls Colne.

By June 1943, the 95th BG, equipped with B-17 Flying Fortress bombers had arrived at RAF Horham, becoming the third American unit to be stationed there. The group, latterly nicknamed "The Iron Men of Metz" due to their impressive bombing accuracy, immediately began flying missions over Nazi-occupied Europe. Their tail marking was a black square with a white letter 'B'.

RAF Horham quickly became a bustling hub of activity, with hundreds of American personnel living and working on the base. The local village of Horham also saw significant changes as the Americans brought in modern facilities and amenities, such as a cinema and a base exchange. Despite the challenges of operating in a foreign land, the USAAF at RAF Horham proved to be a formidable force against the Axis powers. The base was involved in numerous crucial missions, including the bombing of German ball-bearing factories in Schweinfurt, the oil refineries in Ploiești, Romania, and the U-Boat yard at Kiel, as we will discover next.

On June 13, 1943, the group was leading the 4th Bombardment Wing in an attack on U-Boat yards in Kiel, Germany. The lead aircraft carried Brigadier (Brig) General Nathan B. Forrest as an observer. The aircraft was hit by fighters on its approach to the target, and again after the bomb run was complete. It was last seen spiraling out of control, with much of its tail shot away. General Forrest was the first United States general officer killed in action in Europe during the war. The group lost ten aircraft on that raid, their biggest single loss of the war. Interestingly, Brig Forrest had trialed a new formation that day, abandoning the normal 'combat box' for a 'flat formation' with B-17s flying wingtip to wingtip. After the losses that day, it was never flown again.[1]

The group's commitment to mission success was matched by its innovation in tactics and leadership in air combat. Notably, the 95th BG played a pivotal role in developing combat box formation tactics, which improved defensive capabilities and increased bombing accuracy. These formations allowed for more effective protection against enemy fighters and enhanced the overall impact of bombing raids.

The unit flew its last combat mission, an attack on marshalling yards at Oranienburg, on April 20, 1945. On May 7, 1945, the 95th flew a 'Chowhound' mission over German-occupied Holland. These missions, to drop supplies and food to Dutch civilians in German-occupied territory, were carried out by the RAF and USAAF, with the German authorities having given safe passage to these humanitarian flights. On

---

1. https://www.andreaszapf.de/blog-chronicles-media/USAAF-Mission-63-Bremen-and-Kiel.pdf

the return leg, B-17G 44-48640 overflew the Dutch port of IJmuiden, which was then a German E-boat base, and was fired on by an SS machine gun unit, which scored hits on the aircraft, including the No. 2 engine, which caught fire. The aircraft went down in the sea about three and a half miles off Southwold, Suffolk. Of the eight crew members and five passengers on board, there were only four survivors.[2]

As the war in Europe came to an end, the USAAF scaled back its operations at RAF Horham and the base was handed back to the RAF in 1945. The USAAF gave its Stars and Stripes HQ flag to the nearby Stradbroke Church. In later years, the RAF Bloodhound missile site used part of the airfield, but when this was moved, the complete site was sold during 1961-64. Today, RAF Horham is no longer an active military base, but the remains of the airfield can still be seen. The control tower and several buildings have been restored, and there is a memorial to the American servicemen who served there during World War II. The base's contribution to the war

---

2. https://military-history.fandom.com/wiki/RAF_Horham

effort and the sacrifices made by the American personnel will always be remembered and honored.

RAF Thorpe Abbotts

The history of RAF Thorpe Abbotts and the 100th BG is intertwined and reflects the close partnership between the USAAF and the RAF during World War II. Located in south-eastern Norfolk, RAF Thorpe Abbotts served as a base for the USAAF's 100th BG, also known as the "Bloody Hundredth" due to their high casualty rate.

The 100th BG was activated on June 1, 1942, at Orlando Army Air Base in Florida. It was initially assigned to the VIII Bomber Command of the USAAF's Eighth Air Force, but due to the shortage of airfields in England, the group spent the first few months training in the United States. On June 9, 1943 the 100th BG arrived in England from Kearney, AAF, Nebraska, and was stationed at RAF Thorpe Abbotts. The 100th BG tail code was a black square with a white letter 'D'.

The airfield at RAF Thorpe Abbotts was originally built by the RAF in 1942/43 and was used by the

RAF as a satellite airfield for RAF Horham. When the USAAF took over the base in 1943, they made significant improvements to accommodate the heavy B-17 Flying Fortress bombers of the 100th BG. The runway was extended and hardened, and new hangars, barracks, and support facilities were built.

The 100th BG's first combat mission took place on June 25, 1943, when it participated in a bombing raid on Bremen, Germany. The group's primary mission was to attack industrial and military targets in Nazi-occupied Europe, including oil refineries, aircraft factories, and transportation hubs. They also provided support for the D-Day landings in June 1944 and the Allied advance into Germany in 1945.

The 100th BG faced heavy resistance from German fighter planes and anti-aircraft fire during their missions. Their first major battle came on August 17, 1943, during the infamous Schweinfurt-Regensburg mission. The group tragically lost eleven of their twenty-one planes and crew members, with the surviving crews later landing in Algeria after a long flight as part of a wider deception leg. This mission earned them the nickname "Bloody Hundredth." This mission highlighted the dangers of deep penetration raids without adequate fighter escort during the early phase of the USAAF's strategic bombing campaign. Despite the heavy losses, the group continued to fly missions and earned the DUC for their bravery and determination.

Bremen, October 8, 1943

The mission to Bremen was another brutal encounter for the 100th BG, where it again suffered substantial losses. The group's bombers were heavily attacked by German fighters and flak, demonstrating the hazardous environment over heavily defended German targets. Across the 3rd AD, thirty bombers and three fighters were lost that day.

Munster, October 10, 1943

Just two days after the Bremen raid, the 100th BG was tasked with a mission to Munster. This mission became one of the costliest for the group in terms of aircraft and personnel losses in a single day. Specifically, the 100th BG lost twelve of its B-17 Flying Fortresses, representing a significant portion of the aircraft dispatched on the mission, and marking a profound loss in material and, more importantly, in crew members. Each B-17 carried a crew of ten men, meaning the group potentially suffered the loss of up to 120 airmen in terms of killed, captured, or missing during just this single operation.

<u>Berlin Missions, 1944</u>

The 100th BG participated in several missions over Berlin, the capital of Nazi Germany, in 1944. These missions were among the most heavily defended targets due to their political and industrial significance. The 100th's involvement in these raids further solidified its reputation for courage and tenacity under fire. Like other units, aircrews not only faced danger in the air but also from Germans on the ground. On July 29, 1944, during a mission to bomb the Leuna oil refinery near Merseburg, Germany—a critical target due to its contribution to the German war effort—bombers from the 100th BG encountered intense anti-aircraft fire and swarms of Luftwaffe fighters.

Several aircraft were shot down during the raid yet some crew members were able to bail out before the aircraft impacted the ground. Airmen who parachuted from their crippled aircraft should have been protected under the laws of war, as ratified by the (then extant) 1929 Geneva Convention for the protection of prisoners of war. However, in some instances, these norms were brutally violated. On July 29th, 1944, captured crew members from the 100th BG were instead brutally shot by German civilians and military personnel rather than being taken as prisoners.

Such incidents were sadly not isolated to the 100th BG's experience above, rather it represented a wider pattern of atrocities that occurred in the latter part of the war, as Allied bombing intensified and Nazi Germany became increasingly desperate. The murder of downed airmen by civilians or the military outside of combat was a clear violation of the laws of war. These acts were sometimes driven by Nazi propaganda, which portrayed Allied aircrews as "terror flyers," particularly after raids that resulted in high civilian casualties. This propaganda, combined with the stress and devastation of constant bombing, led to a breakdown of the norms of warfare and resulted in acts of vigilante violence against captured airmen.

After the war, some of those responsible for the murder of Allied airmen were tried and convicted in war crimes trials, with many perpetrators being hanged. However, the chaos of the war's end and the sheer scale of the conflict meant that many such crimes went unpunished. The events of July 29, 1944, and similar incidents remain somber reminders of the war's darkest aspects, beyond the conventional battles and campaigns. The 100th BG's sacrifice and the tragic fate of some of its members highlight the complexities and horrors of air warfare in World War II. It underscores the importance of remembrance and the need to uphold the laws of armed conflict to prevent such atrocities from occurring in future conflicts.

By the end of the war, the 100th BG had flown 306 combat missions and dropped over 19,000 tons of bombs. They also held the highest number of missions flown and tonnage dropped by any Eighth Air Force bomb group. However, this success came at a high cost. The group lost 177 aircraft and 732 crew members during their time in Europe. After the war, the 100th BG returned to the United States and was deactivated in November 1945. RAF Thorpe Abbotts was returned to the RAF and carried on as an operational unit and training facility until its eventual closure in 1956.

Today, the site of RAF Thorpe Abbotts is a memorial to the 100th BG and the brave men who served there. The control tower and several buildings have been restored, and a museum has been established to honor the group's legacy. The airfield's main runway is still in use as a private airstrip, and a memorial garden has been created to remember the 100th BG's fallen airmen.

The crews of the 100th epitomize the relentless determination and valor of the USAAF. Their perseverance and resilience in the face of such harrowing adversity made a monumental contribution to the erosion of the Luftwaffe's fighter force and the weakening of the German war machine.

The 100th Air Refueling Wing

The legacy of the 100th BG is preserved by the 100th Air Refueling Wing (ARW), which is today still stationed in East Anglia, 40 miles west of RAF Thorpe Abbotts at RAF Mildenhall. The 100th ARW is the USAF's only permanent air refueling wing in the European theater, and it proudly carries the heritage of the "Bloody Hundredth" in its missions and operations. The squadron currently flies the KC-135 Stratotankers, which all display the large 100th heritage black square and white 'D' on their tails.

5. RAF *Thorpe Abbotts from the air*, 1946

RAF Framlingham

Another airfield established by the USAAF in eastern England was RAF Framlingham, also located in Suffolk. RAF Framlingham was built in 1942 as a Class A bomber base with three concrete runways and multiple hangars. It was initially used by the RAF and the Royal Canadian Air Force (RCAF) for training purposes. However, in early 1943, the USAAF took over the airfield and designated it as Station 153.

The first USAAF unit to arrive at RAF Framlingham was the 95th BG, equipped with B-17 Flying Fortress bombers.

The arrival of the USAAF at RAF Framlingham brought new energy to the airfield. The American airmen were known for their boldness and determination, and they quickly made their presence known. The sound of B-17s taking off and landing became a familiar one in the surrounding countryside. The local villagers were both fascinated and apprehensive about the new arrivals, but they welcomed them with open arms, providing them with supplies and support as they prepared for their missions over Europe.

As the war raged on, the activities at RAF Framlingham only intensified. The 95th BG left in 1943 for RAF Horham, and the 390th BG arrived as Framlingham's new residents, which together with the 100th BG at RAF Thorpe Abbotts, formed the 13th Combat Bombardment Wing. Their tail marking was a black square with the white letter 'J'.

The airfield became a hub of activity, with ground crews working tirelessly to maintain the B-17s and pilots undergoing rigorous training. The airmen knew the risks involved in their missions, but they were determined to do their part in the war effort. Despite the constant threat of enemy attacks and the loss of many brave airmen, RAF Framlingham continued to serve as a vital base for the USAAF. Its strategic location allowed for quick and efficient missions over Europe, and its dedicated personnel played a crucial role in the eventual Allied victory.

One of the group's most notable contributions was its participation in "Big Week" (Operation Argument) in February 1944, which was a series of massive bombing raids against German aircraft production facilities. This operation marked a turning point in the air war over Europe, significantly reducing the Luftwaffe's capacity to defend against Allied air operations and paving the way for the invasion of Normandy. The 390th's efforts during this period were instrumental in achieving air superiority over the continent.

The group also played a vital role in supporting the D-Day invasion on June 6, 1944, by bombing German coastal defenses and transportation networks to disrupt enemy movements and facilitate the Allied ground forces' advance. The 390th BG faced its biggest single day loss of nine aircraft on mission 792 in Germany. Throughout its service, the 390th BG demonstrated exceptional courage and determination, facing formidable defenses and sustaining significant losses in pursuit of their objectives. In over 300 missions, they dropped 19,000 tons of bombs. They lost 181 aircraft, and 714 airmen were killed. Notably, the group also dropped food supplies to the Dutch during the week prior to Victory in Europe Day, proving their worth as not just bombers, but humanitarians too.

The 390th Bomb Group flew its last combat mission on April 20, 1945. After the war, the legacy of the 390th BG continued through its veterans and the establishment of the 390th Memorial Museum in Tucson, Arizona, which honors the group's service and sacrifices. The museum serves as a reminder of the pivotal role played by the 390th BG and other bomber groups in achieving victory in Europe, and the enduring spirit of those who served in the skies above Nazi-occupied Europe.

After the war, RAF Framlingham was initially used as a repatriation center for soldiers returning from overseas, plus a clearing station for the rehabilitation of Polish nationals. The base was finally abandoned in late 1948 and the land was returned to agriculture. The runways were broken up and ground into aggregate. Buildings were allowed to dilapidate. Among them was the Control Tower, which was reportedly shot up and abandoned after the Americans held a riotous farewell party there in August 1945. [3]

Today, remnants of the airfield still stand as a memorial to the bravery and sacrifice of the men and women who served there during World War II. In 1976, a project was undertaken to restore the derelict control tower. The tower was finally dedicated as the '390th BG Memorial Air Museum of the USAAF' on May 13, 1981. Since then, the museum has remained in active contact with US veterans and their families, and receives steadfast support from many supporters and friends. [4]

6. The 390th Bomb Group's control tower at Framlingham, Suffolk, England (Station 153) on May 22, 1944

Chapter 4
The 45th Combat Bombardment Wing

RAF Deopham Green

RAF Deopham Green, also known as USAAF Station 142, was an RAF station located near the town of Hingham in Norfolk, England (incidentally, the birthplace of Samuel Lincoln, President Abraham Lincoln's great-grandfather). The airfield was originally constructed in 1942 as a satellite station for RAF Old Buckenham, which was located approximately six miles south. RAF Deopham Green consisted of three runways, with the main one running 6,000 feet long and equipped with two T-2 hangars and fifty hardstands. The airfield was initially used by the RAF for training purposes, but in 1943, it was transferred to the USAAF and became a key base for the 3rd Bombardment Division.

7. Airmen of the 452nd Bomb Group with their B-17 Flying Fortress (serial number 42-192622) nicknamed "Borrowed Time"

Each bombardment wing of the 3rd AD consisted of three BGs. RAF Deopham Green served as the base for the 452nd BG of the 45th Bombardment Wing. The 452nd BG arrived at RAF Deopham Green in January 1944, bringing with them the B-17 Flying Fortress, a four-engined heavy bomber. The group's primary mission was to support the Allied ground forces by bombing strategic targets such as oil refineries, aircraft factories, and transportation hubs in Germany, France, and the Low Countries. Their tail marking was a black square with a white letter 'L'. The 452nd BG flew a total of 250 combat missions from RAF Deopham Green, with the first one taking place on February 5, 1944. On this mission, the group successfully bombed an aircraft factory in Leipzig, Germany, despite encountering heavy enemy resistance. The group's most notable mission was on June 6, 1944, when they participated in the D-Day invasion by bombing German coastal defenses.

Throughout the war, the 452nd BG faced numerous challenges and losses. The largest single-day loss for the 452nd BG came on May 12 1944 during a bombing run on a fuel depot in Brux, Belgium. Of the seventy-four aircraft launched from the division that day, the 452nd BG lost fourteen. During their valuable contribution to the war effort, the 452nd BG sadly lost 158 aircraft and 550 crew members while stationed at RAF Deopham Green. The 452nd BG received numerous commendations and awards for their bravery and accomplishments, including the Presidential Unit Citation for their role in the D-Day invasion. The 452nd BG was also awarded a DUC for bombing a fighter base at Kaltenkirchen, northern Germany, on April 7, 1945, while under intense pressure from enemy fighters and anti-aircraft flak.

In addition to their bombing missions, the 452nd BG played a significant role in Operation Chowhound on May 1st, 1945, a humanitarian effort to drop food supplies to the Dutch population who were facing famine as a result of the German occupation. The group dropped over 2,000 tons of food to the Dutch, earning them the nickname "The Flying Dutchmen".

When the war came to an end in 1945, RAF Deopham Green was returned to the RAF in November of that year. The 452nd BG was deactivated, and the airfield was used for storage and disposal of surplus equipment until it was eventually closed in 1948. Today, the site of RAF Deopham Green is marked by a memorial plaque and a few remaining buildings, on the airfield's periphery. A small portion of the main runway remains at the western end of the site, near where the road from Hingham to Deopham takes a sharp turn (shown in the image below). The airfield has since been returned to agricultural use, but the legacy of the 452nd BG and their incredible contributions to the fighting tyranny will never be forgotten.

8. What's left of the main runway at RAF Deopham Green in Feb 2024, towards the western end of the old airfield site. (author)

RAF Knettishall

RAF Knettishall, located in Suffolk, also played a vital role as a base for USAAF bomber squadrons of the Eighth Air Force. Activated in 1942, RAF Knettishall (Station 136) became operational in 1943 and was strategically positioned to facilitate long-range bombing missions over occupied Europe and Germany, allowing American bombers to penetrate deep into enemy territory.

One of the notable units stationed at RAF Knettishall was the 388th BG (Heavy). Their tail marking was a black square with a white letter 'H'. The 388th operated Boeing B-17 Flying Fortress bombers, the truly iconic aircraft renowned for their role in daylight precision bombing raids. The group consisted of the 560th, 561st, 562nd, and 563rd Bomb Squadrons. The 388th BG's first combat mission on July 17, 1943, targeting railway yards in Hamm, Germany, marked the beginning of its operational contribution to the strategic bombing campaign. This mission introduced the group to the brutal realities of war over Europe, including intense anti-aircraft fire and the constant threat of enemy fighters.

One of the most famous missions involving the 388th was the daylight raid on the Messerschmitt aircraft factories in Regensburg, Germany, on August 17, 1943. This mission was part of a double-strike plan, with another force targeting the ball-bearing plants in Schweinfurt. The Regensburg mission was a long-range operation pushing the limits of the B-17's capabilities and requiring precise execution. The bombers faced fierce resistance, but the mission significantly impacted the German aircraft production capability. The 388th BG's participation in this raid demonstrated their ability to execute complex and hazardous operations. The group earned a DUC for its outstanding performance during the mission. Despite heavy opposition and sustaining significant damage, the group pressed on to successfully complete its mission, demonstrating exceptional courage and determination.

On September 6, 1943 the 388th fielded twenty-four B-17s to attack a target in Stuttgart. Eighteen aircraft of the larger attack element failed to return, with eleven belonging to the 388th BG. Aircrew losses stood at thirty-nine killed in action (KIA), eighty-four POW, and twenty-nine interned. In addition, two airmen were KIA and thirteen wounded in aircraft that managed to recover back to England. [1]

RAF Knettishall's facilities included hangars, control towers, and other structures necessary for the maintenance and operation of the B-17 fleet. The airfield was a bustling center of activity, with ground crews working diligently to prepare the aircraft for their perilous missions. Support units, responsible

---

1. https://www.americanairmuseum.com/archive/mission/viii-bomber-command-91

for logistics, intelligence, and administrative functions, played an essential role in the overall functioning of the base. The 388th flew 306 missions, and lost a total of 191 aircraft with 524 aircrew KIA. They mounted 8,051 sorties, and were accredited with 222 enemy aircraft kills.

Following the end of hostilities in Europe in May 1945, RAF Knettishall's wartime role came to an end. The airfield was placed in care and maintenance status before being returned to civilian use.

9. B-17F "Tom Paine" of the 388th Bomb Group, RAF Knettishall, England, World War II

RAF Snetterton Heath

RAF Snetterton Heath, located in Norfolk, holds an important place in the archives of World War II aviation history. Constructed in 1943, this airfield became a crucial part of the Allied air campaign against Nazi Germany.

The airfield was originally built to RAF specifications for bomber operations, featuring the classic three-runway A-frame layout prevalent in many British airfields of the era. Once again, its strategic location in England's east made it an ideal point from which heavy bombers could launch missions into the heart of occupied Europe.

The primary tenant of RAF Snetterton Heath during the war was the 96th BG (Heavy), which arrived in the spring of 1943. The 96th BG was part of the 45th Combat Bombardment Wing of the 3rd AD, and it operated the Boeing B-17 Flying Fortress.

The group was composed of four squadrons: the 337th, 338th, 339th, and 413th Bombardment Squadrons. Their tail code was a black square with a white letter 'C'.

These units carried out some of the Eighth Air Force's most critical bombing missions over Germany and Nazi-occupied territories, targeting industrial complexes, military installations, and infrastructure critical to the Axis war effort.

The 96th BG's operations included participation in the infamous Regensburg and Schweinfurt raids, where they encountered fierce resistance from Luftwaffe fighters and intense anti-aircraft fire, highlighting the perilous nature of daylight bombing missions.

Throughout its tenure at Snetterton Heath, the 96th BG demonstrated remarkable bravery and skill, earning two DUCs for their precision and determination under fire.

Their missions contributed significantly to the Allied strategy of crippling Germany's ability to wage war, focusing on disrupting the Luftwaffe's production capacity, degrading the Nazi war machine's logistics and transportation networks, and supporting ground operations following the D-Day landings in Normandy.

The 96th BG participated in the first American daylight bombing raid on Berlin, marking a significant milestone in the air war over Europe. This mission demonstrated the Allies' ability to hit the heart of the German Reich and was a morale booster for Allied forces. It also underscored the strategic shift towards targeting German capital and industrial centers.

The mission was highly dangerous due to the long distance deep into enemy territory, the intense anti-aircraft fire, and the Luftwaffe's determined fighter opposition. The German synthetic fuel plants at Brüx in southern Germany (post-war Most, Czechoslovakia), Lüna-Merseburg, Lützkendorf, and Zeitz in eastern Germany, were hit by 800 US bombers on May 12, 1944. The 96th BG lost twelve B-17s that fateful day.

The airfield at Snetterton Heath underwent several modifications throughout the war to accommodate the needs of its inhabitants and the evolving tactics of the air campaign. These included the construction of additional hardstands to park aircraft, the expansion of runway lengths to handle heavily-loaded bombers, and the improvement of maintenance and operational facilities to ensure the bombers' readiness for mission demands.

The base also hosted a range of support personnel, including ground crews, engineers, medics, and administrative staff, who all played an essential role in the operational success of the 96th BG.

As the war progressed and the Allies gained air superiority over Western Europe, RAF Snetterton Heath continued to serve as a launch point for missions aimed at supporting ground forces, attacking enemy troop concentrations, and harassing retreating German units. These operations were crucial in the final push towards Germany, contributing to the eventual Allied victory in Europe.

After the war, RAF Snetterton Heath was returned to the RAF in July 1945, and its runways eventually fell silent as military operations wound down.

In the post-war years, the airfield was repurposed for civilian use and became well known as a motor racing circuit, preserving the future of RAF Snetterton Heath in a different form. Yet, the bravery and sacrifices of the airmen who flew from its runways during World War II remain the most enduring legacy of this historic airfield.

10. B-17G-70-BO *Flying Fortress* Serial 43-37683, of the 339th Bomb Squadron, 96th Bombardment Group, at RAF Snetterton Heath, England

Chapter 5
The 93rd Combat Bombardment Wing

RAF Mendlesham

RAF Mendlesham, located in Suffolk, played a noteworthy role in the history of the USAAF during World War II. Construction of RAF Mendlesham began in 1942, and it became operational in 1943. The 34th BG, which arrived equipped with B-24 Liberator bombers in April 1944, was the primary unit to be stationed there. The group consisted of four squadrons: the 7th, 18th, 391st, and 392nd Bomb Squadrons. The base was also home to the 93rd Bombardment Wing HQ. The B-24s were known for their long range and high payload capacity, making them highly suitable for strategic bombing missions.

The 34th BG entered combat in May 1944 and continued to participate in numerous missions throughout the war, targeting industrial sites, military installations, and transportation networks in Germany and Nazi-occupied territories. The B-24s and B-17s of the 34th BG became a familiar sight as they launched in their masses for strategic bombing missions, forming up in the skies over East Anglia. Their tail code was a black square with a white letter 'S'.

During this period, the group also supported ground forces during the Battle of the Bulge from December 1944 to January 1945. In March 1945, with few enemy industrial targets remaining and Allied armies advancing across Germany, the 34th BG turned almost solely to interdicting enemy communications and supporting Allied ground forces.

As training programs in the States accelerated, replacement crews arriving later in the war tended to be younger than those arriving earlier. One 34th BG crew, that of 2nd Lt Joe Novick, was claimed to be the youngest in VIII Bomber Command. Lt. Novicki was the "old man" at 21 and all the other crew members were 19 or 20 years old in 1945. The

34th BG flew its last combat mission on April 20, 1945.[1] One of the most incredible feats of the 34th was the fact they did not lose a single bomber to enemy fighter action over enemy territory!

Following the end of hostilities in Europe in May 1945, RAF Mendlesham's wartime role came to an end, and the airfield was placed in care and maintenance status before being returned to the RAF in 1948.

RAF Great Ashfield

RAF Great Ashfield, located in Suffolk, was built in 1942 as a satellite airfield for the nearby RAF Bury St. Edmunds (RAF Rougham). However, in September of the same year, the airfield was transferred to the USAAF and became known as Station 155. The airfield was a Class A airfield with three intersecting concrete runways, a control tower, and a number of hangars and support buildings.

---

1. https://en.wikipedia.org/wiki/34th_Training_Wing#World_War_II

The primary mission of RAF Great Ashfield was to provide support for the Eighth Air Force and ended up as home to the 385th BG, which was part of the 93rd Combat Bombardment Wing. Their tail marking was a black square with a white letter 'G'.

The first 385th BG mission from RAF Great Ashfield took place on October 9, 1942, when a group of B-17s attacked a target in Lille, France. The biggest single day loss for the unit came on October 6, 1944 when attacking Munich; ten aircraft were sadly lost. Over the next two years, the base would see numerous combat assignments, with the 385th BG flying over 300 missions and dropping over 16,000 tons of bombs on enemy targets.

The group led the famous attack on the Focke-Wolfe aircraft factory at Marienburg on October 9, 1943, during which only two out of one hundred B-17s were lost, and all of the buildings on the site were damaged or destroyed. As a result, they won two DUCs. The first was awarded for accurately dropping their payload on an aircraft factory at Regensburg on August 17, 1943, and the group's second was awarded after leading a difficult, long-range mission to destroy aircraft repair works at Zwickau, southwest Germany, on May 12, 1944. [2]

RAF Great Ashfield also played a crucial role in the D-Day invasion of Normandy in June 1944. In the months leading up to the invasion, the base was used as a staging area for the 385th BG as well as other units. On D-Day itself, the base's B-17s were among the first aircraft to fly over the Normandy beaches, providing crucial air support for the Allied troops on the ground.

After the war, RAF Great Ashfield was returned to the RAF and was used as a storage depot for surplus equipment. In 1948, the airfield was closed and returned to agricultural use. Today, little remains of the base, although some of the runways and support buildings can still be seen.

11. Aerial photograph of Great Ashfield airfield 31 March 1944. Photograph taken by 7th Photographic Reconnaissance Group, sortie number US/7PH/GP/LOC264. English Heritage (USAAF Photography).

RAF Eye

RAF Eye is a former World War II airfield located in Suffolk. Construction at RAF Eye began in 1942 and the airfield was officially opened on April 1, 1943. It was predominantly used as a satellite airfield for RAF Horham, which was located just 6 miles away. The airfield was equipped with three concrete runways and a number of dispersal areas for aircraft. It also had a control tower, hangars, and other support buildings.

The first unit to be based at RAF Eye was the No. 149 Squadron RAF, which operated the Avro Lancaster bomber. The squadron was involved in many bombing operations over Germany and played an important role in the famous "Dambusters" raid in May 1943.

The squadron remained at RAF Eye until October 1943 before moving to RAF Methwold in Norfolk. In November 1943, the USAAF's 490th BG arrived at RAF Eye from its base in Salt Lake City, Utah. Their tail marking consisted of a black square with a white letter 'T'.

Initially equipped with B-24 Liberators, the group began its combat operations in June 1944, of which early missions included bombing strategic targets such as oil refineries, railway junctions, and airfields across Nazi-occupied Europe. These operations aimed to cripple the German war machine's logistics and production capabilities, contributing significantly to the Allied effort to gain air superiority over the continent.

In late 1944, the 490th BG underwent a significant transition, re-equipping with the B-17 Flying Fortress, a change that reflected the USAAF's broader strategy shift and operational requirements. The B-17, with its renowned durability and defensive armament, allowed the 490th to undertake precision daylight bombing missions with increased effectiveness.

The group's operations extended to hitting targets deeper into Germany, including industrial complexes, military installations, and urban centers critical to the Nazi war effort. Throughout its service, the 490th BG exemplified the strategic importance of air power in World War II. Its missions contributed to the destruction of vital enemy infrastructure, the disruption of German supply lines, and support for ground forces during critical phases of the European campaign.

The group's successful adaptation to different aircraft and mission profiles underscored the flexibility and resilience of the group. Throughout its time at RAF Eye, the 490th flew a total of 157 missions and dropped over 15,000 tons of bombs, earning numerous awards and commendations for its valiant contributions.

After the war, the 490th BG's legacy continued through its designation in the post-war United States Air Force. With the war over, Eye transferred to RAF Bomber Command on November 1, 1945, as an active station. However, the airfield was gradually run down and was finally sold by the Air Ministry in 1962-63.

With the end of military control, Eye Airfield was converted into an industrial estate, with a large factory for processing straw established in the hangars and former technical site. Later, other industrial developments occurred, and new buildings were built in the same area.

There is now a natural gas pumping station in the center of the former airfield along with major trucking companies using the site as a hub for international transport operations. The airfield and its units will always hold a significant place in the history of the war and the brave individuals who served there.

12. Aerial photograph of Eye Airfield, looking north, 16 July 1943. Photograph taken by 7th Photographic Reconnaissance Group, sortie number US/7PH/GP/LOC2. English Heritage (USAAF Photography).

RAF Debach

RAF Debach, located in Suffolk, was one of the many airfields used by the USAAF during World War II. It played an important role in the air war against Nazi Germany and was home to several USAAF units, including the famous 493rd BG. The airfield was built in 1942 by the RAF as part of the expansion of their bomber force. However, in 1943, it was handed over to the USAAF and became known as Station 152. The USAAF made significant changes to the airfield, including extending the runways and constructing new hangars and barracks to accommodate the larger American aircraft. The first USAAF unit to arrive at RAF Debach was the 493rd BG, also known as the "Helton's Hellcats", in April 1944. Their tail code was a black square with a white letter 'X'. It was the last bombardment group to be formed as part of the Eighth Air Force. The group consisted of four squadrons – the 860th, 861st, 862nd, and 863rd – each equipped with B-17 Flying Fortress bombers.

The 493rd BG flew its first combat mission on May 7, 1944. The target for this mission was the marshalling yards at Kortrijk, Belgium. Marshalling yards were key transportation hubs where trains were assembled and loaded, making them strategic targets for disrupting enemy logistics and transportation networks. The mission aimed to hamper German military capabilities and support the overall Allied strategic bombing campaign in preparation for the Normandy invasion, which took place on June 6, 1944 (D-Day). The group went on to fly a further 156 bombing missions, targeting a range of strategic locations in Germany and tactical targets in northern France, Holland, and along the Rhine. Their final contributions were six resupply missions in May 1945, dropping over 400 tonnes of food into newly liberated parts of Europe.

The airfield at RAF Debach was not without its share of dangers. In March 1944, a B-17 from the 493rd BG crashed on takeoff due to engine failure, killing all on board. In June of the same year, a German V-1 flying bomb landed near the airfield, causing significant damage to buildings and injuring several personnel. The rocket was launched from the Netherlands, likely targeting Ipswich but landing short.

Despite the dangers, RAF Debach continued to play a vital role in the USAAF's air campaign against Germany. The base and its personnel received several commendations for their efforts, including the DUC for their participation in the bombing of the German oil refineries at Politz in August 1944. In addition to its military operations, RAF Debach, like the other American bases, had a significant impact on the local community. The American presence brought a boost to the local economy, with many local businesses benefiting from the influx of American personnel. The airfield also had a social and cultural impact, with dances, concerts, and other events organized for the American servicemen stationed there. After the war, RAF Debach was returned to the RAF and was used as a storage depot for surplus military equipment. In 1946, it was closed and returned to agricultural use. Today, the only reminder of the airfield's wartime past is a small memorial and a few scattered buildings.

13. Formation of 493rd Bombardment Group, B-17 Flying Fortresses at 27,900 Ft, over Schleissmen, Germany 9 April 1945

Chapter 6
The Bomber Aircraft of the 3rd Air Division

The aircraft of the 3rd AD of the US Eighth Air Force, emerged as symbols of hope, defiance, and technological prowess. Operating from the aerodromes of England, these flying fortresses and liberators soared across the European skies, carrying the weight of the free world's aspirations on their wings.

This chapter introduces the reader to the aircraft that were not just tools of war, but embodiments of human ingenuity and spirit, pivotal in tilting the scales of the conflict. The B-17 Flying Fortress and the B-24 Liberator stood at the forefront of the 3rd AD's arsenal. These aircraft, with their distinctive silhouettes, became icons of the Allied bombing campaign, known for their durability, payload capacity, and the sheer will of those who manned them. Alongside, the emergence of the P-51 Mustang as a long-range escort fighter marked a turning point, providing the bomber crews with a guardian angel against the Luftwaffe's persistent attacks.

Diving into the design and development of these aircraft, this chapter explores how each model was a marvel of its time, crafted from the urgency of war yet forward-thinking in its engineering. The B-17, with its four powerful engines, robust frame, and defensive armament, epitomized the heavy bomber's role in achieving air superiority through strategic bombing. Its counterpart, the B-24, with a higher top speed and greater range, offered the Allies the flexibility to strike deeper into enemy territory, targeting infrastructure, supply lines, and military installations. The mixture of B-24s and B-17s in the 3rd AD presented a number of operational problems, and in early 1944, VIII Bomber Command Headquarters began to draw up plans to standardize the 3rd AD with the Flying Fortress.

Through precision daylight bombing, the 3rd AD played a critical role in crippling the German war machine. The destruction of factories, oil refineries, and transportation networks, along with the relentless degradation of the Luftwaffe's fighter strength, underscored the strategic bombing campaign's importance in undermining the Axis powers' ability to sustain the war. In telling the story of these aircraft, we also delve into the technological advancements and tactical innovations that evolved from the crucible of war.

The development of radar-guided bombing, the use of high-altitude photographic reconnaissance, and the implementation of combat formation tactics are examined, showcasing how the 3rd AD's aircraft were at the forefront of aerial warfare innovation. This chapter invites readers to journey through the clouds of history, to understand the machines that carried the hopes of a generation, and to honor the men who flew them. Through their stories, we gain insight into the aircraft that were not just instruments of destruction but beacons of liberation, playing a pivotal role in securing peace and shaping the modern world.

B-17 Flying Fortress

The B-17 bomber, also known as the 'Flying Fortress', was a heavy bomber aircraft used by the USAAF during World War II. It was a vital part of the 3rd AD, which was responsible for strategic bombing missions in Europe. During the war, the B-17 carried out thousands of bombing runs on German targets and undoubtedly helped to turn the tide of the war in favor of the Allies.

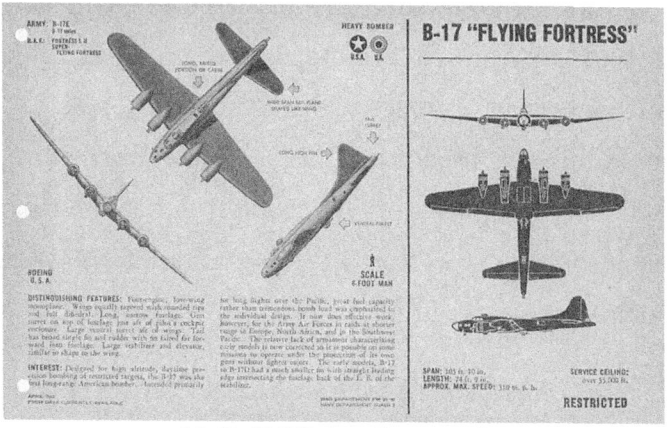

14. B-17 *"Flying Fortress"*

The B-17 was designed and built by the Boeing Company in the late 1930s in response to a request from the United States Army Air Corps for a new long-range bomber. The first prototype flew in July 1935 and was immediately recognized for its impressive performance and capabilities. The B-17 was a four-engine aircraft with a crew of ten and was designed to carry a maximum internal bomb load, which varied depending on the specific B-17 model, but generally ranged from 8,000 to 14,000 pounds of bombs. It had a range of over 2,000 miles and could fly at a maximum speed of 287 miles per hour.

One of the key features of the B-17 was its defensive armament. It had a total of thirteen half inch-caliber machine guns, making it one of the most heavily armed bombers of its time. These guns were positioned in various locations around the aircraft, including the nose, tail, top, and sides, providing 360-degree coverage. This made the B-17 a formidable opponent in the air, as it could defend itself against enemy fighters.

The B-17 was also known for its durability. It was designed to withstand heavy enemy fire and keep flying even with significant damage. This was achieved through the use of a strong and sturdy airframe as well as a self-sealing fuel system that could prevent fires from spreading. The B-17 was also equipped with a backup hydraulic system, which allowed the crew to manually operate the landing gear and flaps in case of damage to the main system.

The success of the B-17 can be attributed to its advanced technology (for the time) and design. It had a highly-innovative and sophisticated Norden bombsight, which allowed for accurate bombing from high altitudes. It also had a pressurized cabin, which meant the crew could operate at high altitudes without the need for oxygen masks. This was important, as it enabled the B-17 to fly above most of the German anti-aircraft fire.

The B-17 was not without its flaws, however. Its heavy armor and armament made it slower and less maneuverable than other aircraft, making it an easy target for enemy fighters. This meant the B-17 ideally needed fighter escorts for protection, and losses were higher when flying without support. Furthermore, the B-17 had a limited range, which meant it could not reach targets in Japan for example, without the use of forward bases.

Despite its limitations, the B-17 played a critical role in the 3rd AD during World War II. It was a reliable and effective aircraft, and its contribution to the Allied victory cannot be overstated. It paved the way for future developments in bomber technology and left a lasting legacy in the history of aviation. The B-17 and its brave crews will always be remembered for their dedication, bravery and sacrifices. The B-17 'Flying Fortress' was more than just a heavy bomber aircraft. It was a symbol of strength, courage, and determination for the Allied forces during World War II. Its powerful engines roared as it took off on countless missions, carrying valiant pilots and crew members who risked their lives for the greater good.

The B-17 was not just a machine but a well-oiled team of individuals working together to achieve a common goal. Each crew member had a specific role and responsibility, and they all depended on each other for survival. From the pilot who skillfully maneuvered the aircraft to the gunners who fiercely defended it from enemy attacks, the B-17 was a true testament to the power of teamwork. But beyond its impressive capabilities and advanced technology, the B-17 had something else that made it stand out—its heart. The men who flew these planes were not just soldiers; they were sons, brothers, husbands, and fathers. They carried the hopes and dreams of their loved ones with them on every mission, and their bravery and sacrifice will never be forgotten. The legacy of the B-17 lives on today as a reminder of the incredible feats that can be achieved when people come together for a common cause. It serves as a symbol of the resilience and determination of the human spirit and will continue to inspire generations to come. The B-17 'Flying Fortress' will always hold a special place in the hearts of those who honor its memory.

Other Allied operators of the B-17 included:

United Kingdom: The B-17 played an important role in the the RAF's bomber arsenal. With over 2,000 B-17 aircraft received through the Lend-Lease program, the British also put them to work in bombing campaigns against Germany. Some were even modified for maritime patrol missions. The RAF squadrons who used the Fortress is listed below:

- No. 59 Squadron RAF, Fortress IIA, from April 1943 to December 1941, based at RAF Thorney Island and RAF Chivenor.

- No. 90 Squadron RAF - Fortress I from 7 May

1941 to February 1942, based at RAF Watton, RAF West Raynham and RAF Polebrook.

- No. 206 Squadron RAF - Fortress II from July 1942 to March 1944, based at RAF Benbecula, RAF Lagens.

- No. 214 Squadron RAF: Fortress II from January 1941 to July 1945 and Fortress III from November 1944 to July 1945, based at RAF Sculthorpe and RAF Oulton.

- No. 220 Squadron RAF - Fortress I from December 1941 to August 1942, Fortress II from July 1942 to December 1944. Based at RAF Wick, RAF Nutts Corner, RAF Ballykelly, RAF Aldergrove, RAF Benbecula, RAF Lagens.

- No. 223 Squadron RAF, Fortress II and III, from April 1945 to July 1945 at RAF Oulton.

- No. 251 Squadron RAF - Fortress II from March 1945 to October 1945 at RAF Reykjavik.

- No. 517 Squadron RAF - Operated USAAF B-17Fs from September to November 1943 at RAF St Eval

- No. 519 Squadron RAF - Fortress II from November 1944 to September 1945 at RAF Wick

- No. 521 Squadron RAF - Fortress II from December 1944 to February 1946, Fortress III from December 1945 to February 1946 at RAF Docking.

Canada: The Royal Canadian Air Force (RCAF) was also no stranger to the B-17 during World War II. With 164 of these planes received through the Lend-Lease program, the RCAF used them for anti-submarine patrols and escorting convoys.

Australia: In the Pacific theater, the Royal Australian Air Force (RAAF) relied on the 287 B-17s provided through the Lend-Lease program for bombing missions against Japanese forces.

Soviet Union: Although seventy-three B-17s were sent to the Soviet Union from the United States through the Lend-Lease program, they were not used for bombing missions. Instead, they were primarily utilized for reconnaissance and transport duties.

Free French Forces: A small number of B-17s were also sent to the Free French Air Force from the United States. These planes were used against multiple targets in German-occupied Europe.

Brazil: During World War II, Brazil received thirteen B-17s through the Lend-Lease program and used them for strategic bombing missions against targets in Italy.

China: The Chinese Air Force also received support from the United States in the form of thirty-seven B-17s through the Lend-Lease program. These planes were used to bomb Japanese targets in China and for transporting supplies and personnel.

Israel: After World War II, Israel purchased twenty-five surplus B-17s from the United States. These planes were used during the 1948 Arab-Israeli War for bombing and reconnaissance missions.

West Germany: Following the war, West Germany acquired a small number of B-17s from the United States. These planes were primarily used for transportation and research purposes.

Argentina: In the late 1940s, the United States provided Argentina with fifteen B-17s. These planes were utilized for military transport and cargo missions.

Nazi Germany: During World War II, after crash landing or being forced down, approximately forty B-17s were repaired and put back into the air by the Luftwaffe. These captured aircraft were codenamed "Dornier Do 200", given German markings, and used for clandestine spy and reconnaissance missions by the Luftwaffe, most often by the Kampfgeschwader 200 unit, hence a likely possibility as a source for the "Do 200" codename.

B-24 Liberator

15. B-24 'Liberator'

The B-24 Liberator was primarily used by the USAAF and the RAF as a long-range bomber capable of carrying heavy loads of bombs to enemy targets, but was also used for reconnaissance, maritime patrol, and transport missions. It became the most produced military aircraft of all time with over 18,000 airframes built. The RAF and French Air Force had submitted their bids for the B-24 even before the aircraft had started rolling off the production lines, and oddly it was the RAF that was the first operator of the Liberator, not the USAAF.

The B-24 Liberator was designed and manufactured by Consolidated Aircraft Corporation, with the first prototype taking flight in 1939. It was designed to be a longer and more powerful version of the B-17 Flying Fortress, with a larger bomb load capacity and longer range. The B-24 had a wingspan of 110 feet and a length of sixty-seven feet, making it one of the largest aircraft of its time. Its design also included a tricycle landing gear, which made it easier to take off and land on rough runways.

One of the key features of the B-24 Liberator was its ability to carry a large bomb load. It had a bomb bay that could hold 12,000 to 20,000 pounds of bombs, making it a highly effective bomber. In terms of maximum total payload (internal + external), the B-24 generally had the advantage over the B-17, often capable of carrying 1,000 to 6,000 pounds (450 to 2,720 kg) more than the Flying Fortress. Another key feature was its ability to fly at high altitudes, making it difficult for enemy fighters to reach. With this increased height though comes reduced bombing accuracy given the varying wind conditions and other weather the bombs might face en-route to their target. The higher operating altitude, combined with its powerful engines and intimidating defensive capabilities, made it a formidable opponent in the air. But beyond its role as a bomber, the B-24 also played a role in other missions, such as reconnaissance and transport, showcasing its versatility and adaptability.

The B-24 was also equipped with ten half-inch caliber machine guns, which provided it with a strong defensive capability against enemy aircraft. The guns were operated by a crew of ten, including the pilot, co-pilot, navigator, bombardier, radio operator, and gunners. The B-24 Liberator was powered by four Pratt & Whitney R-1830 Twin Wasp engines, each producing 1,200 horsepower. These powerful engines gave the B-24 a maximum speed of 290 mph and a cruising speed of 215 mph. It also had a range of 2,100 miles, which made it an ideal aircraft for long-range missions. The B-24 was capable of flying at an impressive maximum altitude of 28,000 feet.

During World War II, the B-24 Liberator was primarily used in the European and Pacific theaters against strategic targets in Germany, Italy. The B-24 played a vital role in the D-Day invasion of Normandy, dropping paratroopers and bombing enemy positions, and in the Pacific, the B-24 was used to bomb Japanese strongholds and supply lines, as well as supporting ground troops during island-hopping campaigns.

The B-24 Liberator also had a significant impact on the Allied victory in the Battle of the Atlantic. It was used for anti-submarine warfare, patrolling the vast expanses of the Atlantic Ocean and hunting for German U-boats. The B-24s would drop depth charges on suspected U-boat locations, making them a key player in the fight against German submarines. The B-24 Liberator's contribution to the war effort did not end with World War II. It continued to serve in various roles with different air forces around the world, including the United States, the United Kingdom, and India. It was also used in the Korean War and played a significant role in the Berlin Airlift. The B-24 was eventually retired from military service in the 1960s, although some were converted for civilian use, such as firefighting and crop dusting.

The B-24 Liberator was a true workhorse of the skies, tirelessly carrying out its duties for nearly three decades. But beyond its impressive specifications, the B-24 was also known for its reliability and durability, making it a favorite among pilots and crew members alike. The B-24, like all aircraft, was not without criticism from some members of the crew, with the main issues listed below:

Lack of Defensive Armament: Some versions of the B-24, particularly early models, were criticized for having fewer defensive guns and less effective defensive firepower compared to the B-17. This made them more vulnerable to enemy fighter attacks, especially during daylight bombing missions.

Operational Altitude: The B-24 was capable of flying at higher altitudes than the B-17, but it was subsequently less maneuverable at due to thinner air. This made it more vulnerable to enemy fighters during bomber formations and in combat situations.

Crew Comfort: Crew comfort and conditions in the B-24 were generally considered to be inferior to those in the B-17. The B-24 had a narrower fuselage, which resulted in less space for crew members and more uncomfortable working conditions during long missions.

Structural Vulnerability: The B-24's design made it more susceptible to structural damage from enemy anti-aircraft fire and fighter attacks. The aircraft's thin fuselage and larger wing area meant a greater risk of catastrophic damage when hit.

Visibility: Some crew members found the B-24's cockpit visibility to be less favorable than that of the B-17, which made it more challenging for pilots to navigate and maintain formation during missions.

The Royal Canadian Air Force (RCAF), with the help of the Lend-Lease program, also utilized the B-24 for anti-submarine operations and bombing missions in Europe. The Royal Australian Air Force

(RAAF) used the B-24 in the South West Pacific theater, employing it for bombing raids against Japanese targets as well as for transport and reconnaissance missions. The Soviet Air Force was another recipient of B-24 Liberators through the Lend-Lease program, using them for transport and reconnaissance missions.

After the liberation of France in 1944, the French Air Force received B-24s who also began flying them in bombing missions against German targets. Similarly, the Brazilian Air Force, Dutch Air Force, Chinese Air Force, Indian Air Force, Polish Air Force, South African Air Force, Hellenic Air Force, Yugoslav Royal Air Force, and Turkish Air Force all had their share of B-24 Liberators, using them for various purposes such as anti-submarine patrols, transport, bombing, and reconnaissance missions.

Despite its retirement from military service, the B-24 Liberator will always hold a special place in the hearts of those who flew and worked on it. Its impact on World War II will forever be remembered as a symbol of American strength and determination in the face of adversity. The B-24 truly was a legend in the skies, and its story will continue to inspire future generations of aviators.

The Norden Bomb Sight

To aid with precision bombing, both the B-17 and B-24 were fitted with a top-secret analog computer called the Norden bombsight, and its story represents a rather fascinating chapter in military aviation history. Developed by Carl L. Norden, a Dutch engineer, in the late 1920s and early 1930s, the Norden bombsight was designed to improve bombing accuracy, enabling aircraft to hit targets from high altitudes with unprecedented precision.

The device's development was shrouded in secrecy, with Norden and his team working under strict security to prevent its details from falling into enemy hands. The bombsight was so valued that bombardiers had to take an oath to protect it with their lives, and it was always removed from the aircraft and locked up when not in use.

The Norden bombsight consisted of a complex series of gears, levels, and a telescope. It calculated the bomb's trajectory based on the airplane's altitude, speed, and direction, allowing the bombardier to make adjustments for wind speed and direction. When aligned correctly, the bombsight theoretically enabled the bomb to be dropped with pinpoint accuracy.

Its involvement in the war became a symbol of American air power. The belief in the Norden bombsight's accuracy was so strong that it was credited with the ability to "drop a bomb into a pickle barrel from 20,000 feet." While this level of precision was more myth than reality, the Norden did significantly improve bombing accuracy under ideal conditions.

Despite its advancements, the effectiveness of the Norden bombsight was limited by factors such as weather, anti-aircraft fire, and the high speeds and altitudes at which bombers operated. Its legendary status was also challenged by the advent of radar and other technologies later in the war.

Nevertheless, the Norden bombsight remains a significant innovation in military technology, emblematic of the era's scientific ingenuity and the intense focus on aerial warfare strategies during World War II. Its development and use marked a pivotal moment in the evolution of precision bombing, influencing post-war military and aviation technology.

The secrecy surrounding the Norden bombsight, while heavily guarded by the United States, was actually compromised during World War II. Despite extensive measures to ensure its security, including the bombardiers' oaths, the technology did not remain exclusively in Allied hands throughout the conflict.

There were multiple instances and allegations of espionage that suggest the Nazis had actually already obtained information about the Norden bombsight. One of the most notable incidents involved Herman W. Lang, a German-born American who worked at the Carl L. Norden, Inc. factory. Lang was later convicted of espionage for smuggling the plans to Germany in 1938 by reportedly hiding them in an umbrella case and handing them over to German authorities.

The revelation that the Nazis had knowledge of the Norden bombsight underscored the challenges of maintaining technological secrecy during wartime. It also highlighted the ongoing battle between espionage and counter-espionage efforts on both sides. However, the Allied forces' ability to adapt and innovate in their strategic bombing campaigns ultimately played a more significant role in the outcome of the war than the compromise of the Norden bombsight's secrecy.

Chapter 7
The VIII Fighter Command

VIII Fighter Command played a critical role in supporting the 3rd AD during World War II and was responsible for providing air cover and protection for the B-17 and B-24s. Their bombing missions were often long and dangerous, as the bombers had to fly deep into enemy territory, facing heavy anti-aircraft fire and enemy fighter planes.

To ensure the success of these missions, the VIII Fighter Command provided fighter escorts for the bombers. This involved flying alongside the bombers, protecting them from enemy attacks, and engaging in air-to-air combat if necessary. The fighter pilots were highly skilled and trained in aerial combat, making them a formidable force against enemy fighters, especially with their vastly superior P-51 Mustang. Initially equipped with P-38 Lightnings and then P-47 Thunderbolts, the P-51 Mustangs began escorting the bombers on a large scale in early 1944, providing effective protection and contributing significantly to the reduction of losses among the bomber crews.

Instead of dedicated units consistently protecting the 3rd AD, the VIII Fighter Command provided dynamic support through various fighter groups, depending on the mission and operational landscape. This evolved throughout the war:

Early War (1942-1943):

- No specific fighter groups were permanently linked to bomber divisions.

- VIII Fighter Command provided escort and top cover for various bomber formations, including the 3rd AD, on a mission-by-mission basis.

Later War (1944 onwards):

- The Eighth Air Force reorganized, assigning fighter wings to specific bomber divisions and creating air divisions. This change occurred in September 1944.

- The 66th Fighter Wing (FW) had already formed in July 1943 from the 5th Air Defense Wing with the specific role of supporting the 3rd AD of the Eighth Air Force.

- Their callsign was 'Oilskin'.

- The main operating bases for the 66th FW were RAF Duxford and later RAF Troston (late 1945) and the 66th FW HQ was located at Sawston Hall.

The 66th Fighter Wing constituent fighter groups were:

- 55th Fighter Group: 14 September 1943 – 23 July 1945 - RAF Wormingford

- 78th Fighter Group: April 1943 – October 1945 - RAF Duxford

- 339th Fighter Group: 4 April 1944 – October 1945 - RAF Fowlmere

- 353d Fighter Group: 3 August 1943 – October 1945 - RAF Raydon

- 357th Fighter Group: 31 January 1944 – 8 July

1945 -RAF Leiston

- 3rd Scouting Force: September 1944 – June 1945 - RAF Wormingford

In addition to providing escort, the VIII Fighter Command also conducted offensive missions, targeting enemy airfields, aircraft, and other strategic targets. These missions helped to weaken the enemy's air defenses and reduce the threat to the 3rd AD. The VIII Fighter Command further played a vital role in conducting reconnaissance missions, gathering intelligence on enemy targets, and providing valuable information to the 3rd AD. This information was crucial in planning and executing successful bombing missions.

The support from the VIII Fighter Command's highly skilled fighter pilots was essential in ensuring the success of the 3rd AD's missions.

Chapter 8
The Fighter Aircraft of the 66th Fighter Wing

The following chapter will look at the VIII Fighter Command aircraft and flying 'Aces' from the era. From the initial P-38 Lightning's that equipped many of the fighter squadrons in the early part of the war, to the P-47s that came in 1943, and later to the P-51 Mustangs that arrived in the last throes of the war, providing battle-winning endurance and escorting the bombers to their targets and back.

P-38 Lightning

The P-38 Lightning, a distinctive aircraft with its twin-boom design and central nacelle containing the cockpit and armament, emerged as a versatile and formidable fighter during World War II. Developed by Lockheed, the P-38 was unique among

American fighters of the era due to its configuration, allowing it to undertake a variety of missions including reconnaissance, escort, and ground attack.

16. The P-38 Lightning

The VIII Fighter Command, part of the Eighth Air Force, was established to support the bombing campaign against Nazi Germany, providing protection to the heavy bombers that were tasked with destroying German military and industrial targets. The P-38 Lightning units within the VIII Fighter Command played an important role in this endeavor, offering a blend of speed, firepower, and range that was unmatched by many other fighters of the time. The 55th Fighter Group out of RAF Nuthampstead began operations with Lockheed P-38H Lightnings on October 15, 1943, and was the first to use these aircraft on long-range escort missions from the UK. The P-38H differed from earlier versions as they were powered by two 1425-hp Allison V-1710-89/91 engines.

The P-38 could reach speeds of over 400 mph and had a range of more than 2,000 miles with drop tanks. This made it one of the few fighters capable of escorting bombers from England deep into German-occupied territory and back without refueling. Its armament, consisting of four half-inch-caliber machine guns and a 20mm cannon, all mounted in the nose, allowed for unprecedented firepower directly ahead, making it a deadly adversary in dogfights and a precise strafing platform for ground attacks. It was, however, not an aircraft without problems, especially in the cold European environment.

The P-38 Lightning, while a highly versatile and potent aircraft, encountered several challenges related to serviceability and operations when deployed in the UK. These challenges were influenced by the European theater's unique operational conditions, which differed significantly from those in the Pacific, where the P-38 also served extensively. Some of the notable issues faced by P-38 units in the UK included:

Engine and Supercharger Issues:

The P-38's Allison V-1710 engines were equipped with turbo-superchargers to enhance high-altitude performance. However, in the cold, damp climate of the UK, these engines often suffered from mechanical issues, including difficulties with the superchargers that were critical for maintaining power at high altitudes during escort missions and combat operations. The maintenance of these complex systems in less-than-ideal weather conditions contributed to operational challenges.

Turbocharger Failures:

The P-38's turbocharger system, vital for its high-altitude performance, was prone to reliability issues in the European theater. Failures in this system could significantly reduce the aircraft's effectiveness, limiting its ability to perform at the high altitudes necessary for bomber escort missions over Europe.

Fuel System Vulnerabilities:

The P-38's fuel system was more complex and vulnerable to damage compared to single-engine fighters. This complexity increased the risk of fuel leaks and fires, especially during combat engagements and when subjected to the rigors of long-range missions over enemy territory.

Icing Problems:

The P-38 operated in a wide range of weather conditions over Europe and icing was a significant problem. The aircraft's turbochargers and carburetors were susceptible to icing in the cold, moist conditions prevalent in the European theater, affecting performance and reliability.

Maintenance Challenges:

The P-38's unique design, with its twin booms and central nacelle, required specialized maintenance procedures and knowledge. The scarcity of spare parts and the maintenance learning curve for ground crews not familiar with the aircraft's systems added to the operational challenges. The P-38's complexity compared to single-engine fighters like the P-51 Mustang and P-47 Thunderbolt meant that turnaround times between missions could be longer, impacting sortie rates.

Adaptation to European Operations:

The P-38 was initially designed for the Pacific Theater, where it excelled in long-range missions over vast expanses of ocean. Adapting to the European theater, with its different operational requirements, including the need for high-altitude performance and engagement in more frequent, intense air-to-air combat, highlighted some of the aircraft's limitations. Despite these challenges, the P-38 Lightning made significant contributions to the Allied air effort in Europe. Its pilots adapted to the aircraft's quirks and exploited its strengths, such as its excellent range, firepower, and versatility. Over time, improvements in tactics, maintenance practices, and modifications to the aircraft helped mitigate some of the serviceability issues, allowing the P-38 to remain an important part of the air war until more suitable aircraft for the European theater, like the P-51 Mustang, became available in larger numbers.

Famous P-38 Units

One of the most famous P-38 units within the VIII Fighter Command was the 20th Fighter Group. Stationed at Kings Cliffe, England, the 20th Fighter Group was instrumental in the success of daylight bombing raids over Europe. Pilots of the group painted their aircraft's noses red, earning them the nickname "The Red Noses." The group's P-38s provided critical long-range escort to B-17 and B-24 bombers, engaging Luftwaffe fighters in intense aerial battles and protecting the bombers with their aggressive tactics and superior flying skills.

The 78th Fighter Group (RAF Goxhill and RAF Duxford): Before transitioning to P-47s and later P-51s, the 78th Fighter Group used the P-38 Lightning, especially in the early stages of establishing air superiority over Europe. They exchanged their P-38s for P-47s when transferring to RAF Duxford in April 1943 with the P-38s being transferred to Northern Africa. The Allison V-1710 engines used in the P-38 benefited from the dry, warm conditions of North Africa. These conditions were less likely to cause the mechanical issues and turbocharger problems that plagued the aircraft in the cold, damp climate of the UK. The engines' cooling systems operated more efficiently in the dry air, reducing the risk of overheating and enhancing overall performance.

P-38 Lightning 'Aces'

Richard I. Bong and Thomas McGuire: Richard I. Bong (sadly killed in a test flight accident in 1945) and Thomas McGuire (also killed in a 'controlled flight into terrain,' or CFIT accident in 1945 flying his P-38 into the ground during a dogfight) were two of the most famous P-38 pilots of World War II. Bong was the highest-scoring American ace of the war, with forty aerial victories, while McGuire was the second highest, with thirty-eight victories. Both pilots received the Medal of Honor for their extraordinary combat achievements.

During World War II, several other countries in addition to the United States used the Lockheed P-38 Lightning in various capacities. These countries included:

United Kingdom: The UK received a number of P-38 Lightning aircraft through the Lend-Lease program and the RAF used them primarily for reconnaissance missions.

Soviet Union: The Soviet Union received P-38s through the Lend-Lease program as well, using theirs for reconnaissance and training purposes.

Australia: The Royal Australian Air Force (RAAF) operated P-38s, predominantly for training purposes.

New Zealand: The Royal New Zealand Air Force (RNZAF) also used P-38s for training purposes.

France: After the liberation of France, some P-38 Lightning aircraft were operated by the French Air Force.

Italy: Following the surrender of Italy in 1943, a small number of P-38s were captured and used by the Italian Co-Belligerent Air Force, which fought alongside the Allies.

China: The Chinese Nationalist Air Force (Kuomintang) received P-38s and used them in combat against Japanese forces.

Brazil: The Brazilian Air Force operated P-38s after World War II. While the P-38 Lightning was primarily associated with the USAAF, its versatility and capabilities made it a valuable aircraft that saw service in various countries during and after the war.

The P-38 Lightning's impact on the war effort was not limited to its combat prowess. Its ability to fly higher and faster than many enemy fighters made it an excellent platform for photographic reconnaissance missions. Equipped with cameras instead of weapons, reconnaissance variants of the P-38, known as the F-4 and F-5, provided critical intelligence on enemy positions, movements, and fortifications. This intelligence was vital for planning bombing missions and assessing their effectiveness.

The service of the P-38 Lightning with the VIII Fighter Command in England exemplifies the aircraft's versatility and its contribution to the Allied victory in Europe. Its pilots admired the aircraft for its reliability, performance, and firepower. The P-38 Lightning, through its service in various units of the VIII Fighter Command, left an indelible mark on the air war over Europe, showcasing American industrial ingenuity and the bravery of its pilots.

P-47 Thunderbolt

17. Republic P-47D-2-RA Thunderbolt Serial 42-22548 "Gigs-Up" of the 486th Fighter Squadron, 352d Fighter Group, at RAF Bodney, England.

The P-47 Thunderbolt was a formidable single-seat fighter-bomber aircraft used by the USAAF and RAF, and was primarily designed for ground attack missions. It was one of the largest and heaviest single-engine fighters of its time, and its powerful performance and rugged construction made it a favorite among pilots.

The Thunderbolt was first introduced in 1941 and used extensively throughout the war, particularly in the European and Pacific theaters. It was operated by the VIII Fighter Command of the USAAF, which was responsible for protecting the strategic bombing missions against German targets. The P-47 proved to be an extremely capable aircraft in these missions, and its contribution to the Allied victory cannot be overstated. Designed by Republic Aviation, it was the first USAAF fighter to have a cockpit that was pressurized and air-conditioned, making it comfortable for pilots to fly at high altitudes for extended periods.

One of the key specifications of the P-47 Thunderbolt was its size. It had a wingspan of forty feet and nine inches, and was thirty-six and one inch in length. The height of the aircraft was 14 feet and eight inches. The Thunderbolt was a sturdy and robust aircraft, weighing in at over 12,000 pounds when empty. This made it one of the heaviest fighters of its time, and its weight was attributed to its rugged construction and the powerful Pratt & Whitney R-2800 Double Wasp engine that powered it.

The P-47 was equipped with eight half-inch-caliber machine guns, four in each wing, making it an intimidating opponent in air-to-air combat. It was also capable of carrying up to 2,500 pounds of bombs, rockets, and external fuel tanks, allowing it versatility for ground attack missions. The Thunderbolt's firepower and payload capacity were critical in its role as a fighter-bomber, and it was used effectively to target enemy airfields, railroads, and other strategic targets.

One of the most distinctive features of the P-47 Thunderbolt was its "razorback" design. This referred to the high dorsal spine behind the cockpit, which was necessary to accommodate the large engine. This design gave the Thunderbolt excellent stability and allowed for better control during high-speed dives. However, it also created a blind spot for the pilot, making it vulnerable to attacks from the rear and less suitable for aerial dogfighting. This issue was addressed in later versions of the Thunderbolt; Republic Aviation fitted a bubble canopy from a British Hawker Typhoon onto a P-47D-5-RE in July 1943 which provided much better all-round visibility for the pilot. The bubble top was not given a new designation; instead, it was a continuation of the P-47D line.

In terms of performance, the P-47 was an exceptional aircraft. It had a top speed of over 400 mph and a range of over 1,000 miles, making it a capable long-range fighter. The Thunderbolt was also known for its durability, with its tough construction allowing it to withstand significant damage and still return to base. This made it a favorite among pilots, who dubbed it the "Jug" due to its resemblance to a milk jug. There were, however, some issues with the engines in the cold UK climate:

Engine Maintenance:

The Pratt & Whitney R-2800 Double Wasp was a powerful radial engine; while reliable, this engine required significant maintenance, especially under the harsh operating conditions of the European theater. The cold, damp weather in the UK often necessitated more frequent engine inspections and maintenance to prevent issues such as spark plug fouling and carburetor icing.

Turbocharger System:

Like the P-38 Lightning, the P-47 Thunderbolt also relied on a turbocharger system to enhance its high-altitude performance. While this system was generally reliable, it did require careful maintenance and could be a source of operational issues if not properly attended to. The complex system needed regular checks to ensure it was functioning correctly, particularly given the importance of high-altitude performance during escort missions.

Fuel Consumption:

The P-47's powerful engine and robust build came at the cost of high fuel consumption. This trait limited its range in the early stages of its deployment, posing challenges for long-range escort missions until the introduction of external fuel tanks. The need to manage fuel load and consumption carefully could complicate mission planning and reduce the time the aircraft could spend in combat zones or on patrol.

Size and Weight:

Its large size and weight made it less maneuverable than other fighter aircraft, making it vulnerable to enemy fighters in certain situations. It also had a high landing speed, making it challenging to land on shorter runways.

Nevertheless, the Thunderbolt's impressive firepower and versatility made it a valuable asset in the USAAF's arsenal.

In total, over 15,000 P-47 Thunderbolts were produced, and they remained in service with the USAAF until the end of World War II. The P-47's ruggedness and firepower made it a favorite among pilots and even today, the P-47 Thunderbolt is remembered as one of the most esteemed fighter aircraft of World War II.

P-47 Aces

Colonel Francis S. "Gabby" Gabreski:

Gabby Gabreski was one of the most celebrated American aces of World War II. He scored a total of twenty-eight aerial victories while flying the P-47 Thunderbolt, primarily in the European Theater. Gabreski continued his combat career during the Korean War and became one of the highest-scoring aces in U.S. history.

Captain Robert S. Johnson:

Robert S. Johnson was one of the top P-47 Thunderbolt aces of the war. He achieved twenty-seven confirmed aerial victories during his service, primarily in the European Theater with the 56th Fighter

Group. Johnson's combat achievements earned him the Distinguished Service Cross.

Colonel David C. Schilling:

David Schilling was a P-47 pilot who scored twenty-two aerial victories during the war. He later became the commander of the 56th Fighter Group and played a significant role in the European Theater and the Allied victory over Axis forces.

Major Walker "Bud" Mahurin:

Bud Mahurin was a P-47 pilot with the 63rd Fighter Squadron based at RAF Halesworth, England, who scored twenty-one aerial victories in both the European and Mediterranean theaters. He was known for his aggressive flying style and exceptional marksmanship.

Lieutenant Colonel Joseph H. Laughlin:

Joseph Laughlin was a P-47 Thunderbolt pilot who achieved twenty-one aerial victories during World War II. He was highly regarded for his combat skills and leadership abilities. He served with the 362nd Fighter Group initially at RAF Wormingford, before the group pushed into France and eventually Germany.

Lieutenant Colonel Benjamin S. Preston:

Benjamin Preston was a P-47 pilot who achieved twenty aerial victories during his service in the European theater.

Major Robert L. Baseler:

Robert Baseler was a P-47 Thunderbolt pilot with the 325th Fighter Group operating out of Tunisia and Italy with the Fifteenth Air Force, who achieved fifteen aerial victories during World War II. He was known for his exceptional gunnery skills.

Other allied operators of the P-47 included:

Soviet Union: The Soviet Air Force received more P-47s than any other allied nation, with over 6,000 aircraft delivered under the Lend-Lease program. The Soviet variant was known as the P-47D-22-RE and it was used primarily for ground attack missions.

United Kingdom: The RAF also used the P-47 as a fighter-bomber in the European Theater of Operations. The British variant was designated as the Thunderbolt Mk.I., and it featured a modified cockpit layout and British radio equipment.

France: The Free French Air Force operated P-47s during World War II, with 446 aircraft delivered under the Lend-Lease program. The French variant was known as the Thunderbolt FG.1 and it was used for ground attack missions in the Mediterranean and Western Europe.

China: The Chinese Air Force received a small number of P-47s under the Lend-Lease program. The Chinese variant was designated as the P-47D-40-RA, and it was used for ground attack missions against Japanese forces in China.

Brazil: The Brazilian Air Force also received P-47s under the Lend-Lease program and used them for ground attack missions in the Italian Campaign. The Brazilian variant was known as the F-47C, and it featured a reinforced structure and tropicalized equipment for operations in the Brazilian climate.

Mexico: The Mexican Air Force received a total of twenty-five P-47D-30-RA aircraft under the

Lend-Lease program. These aircraft were used for ground attack and air defense missions.

Australia: RAAF operated a small number of P-47s in the Southwest Pacific Theater. The Australian variant was designated as the Thunderbolt Mk.II, and it featured a shortened tail and a modified wing structure for carrier operations.

Netherlands: The Royal Netherlands Air Force also received P-47s under the Lend-Lease program, with ninety-six aircraft delivered. The Dutch variant was known as the Thunderbolt Mk.I., and it was used for ground attack missions in the Dutch East Indies.

Free Polish Air Force: The Polish Air Force in exile operated P-47s in the Western European Theater. The Polish variant was designated as the P-47D-30-RE, and it featured a larger fuel capacity and improved armor protection.

Greece: The Royal Hellenic Air Force also used P-47s during World War II, with ninety-six aircraft delivered under the Lend-Lease program. The Greek variant was known as the Thunderbolt Mk.II, and it featured a modified canopy and gunsight for better visibility.

In conclusion, the P-47 Thunderbolt was a powerful and robust platform whose size, firepower, and durability made it a menacing opponent in both air-to-air and ground attack missions, and the pilots of the 3rd AD relied heavily on the Thunderbolt to carry out their escort missions with precision and effectiveness.

The P-51 Mustang

The P-51 Mustang is arguably one of the most iconic fighters of World War II. Designed and produced by North American Aviation, it played a decisive role in the war efforts of the Allied forces, particularly in the European theater. The latter P-51 Mustang was a long-range, single-seat fighter aircraft that served primarily in the USAAF and the RAF. It was known for its speed, maneuverability, and endurance, making it a formidable opponent in aerial combat.

18. P-51 Mustangs (CS-E, serial number 44-13893) nicknamed "Caroline", (CS-L, serial number 44-14733) nicknamed "Ruggie's Ruthie", (CS-F, serial number 44-13795) nicknamed "Marg" and (CS-K, serial number 44-13966) of the 359th Fighter Group lined up at East Wretham

The Mustang entered production in May 1941 and began combat operations with the RAF in April 1942. Some 1,579 Allison-powered Mustangs were produced. They were typically equipped with two half-inch-caliber nose-mounted and four third-inch-caliber wing-mounted machine guns, although one model had four, twenty-mm cannons and another (the A-36A) was a dive bomber for the USAAF. They served as low-altitude fighters and as long-range photo-reconnaissance aircraft under the designation F-6, mostly with the RAF.

It soon became apparent that the plane's true potential lay in its ability to escort bombers on long-range missions. It was also highly maneuverable, which gave it an advantage in dogfights against the slower and less agile German fighters. One of the most notable units that flew the P-51 Mustang was the VIII Fighter Command of the USAAF in support of the 3rd AD's daylight precision bombing raids on German targets. The P-51 Mustang proved to be a game-changer for the 3rd AD. With its long-range capabilities, the Mustang was able to accompany the bombers all the way to their targets and back, providing them with much-needed protection. The P-51 pilots were also highly skilled and were able to engage and defeat the German fighters, greatly reducing the losses of the bombers.

The Mustang was initially powered by the Allison V-1710 engine, which was originally designed for use in high-altitude bombers. However, this engine was not well-suited for the Mustang's role as a long-range fighter and had limited range and performance. Early models of the P-51 with Allison engines (P-51A and earlier variants) had carburetors that could cause engine stalling in certain combat maneuvers, such as negative G dives. This was addressed in later models, as we will discover below, with the adoption of the Merlin engine, which used a fuel injection system instead of a carburetor, significantly improving reliability and performance.

The RAF had been experimenting with the Rolls-Royce Merlin engine from the Spitfire fitted to the Mustang and had noted the increased performance. The Merlin was already being produced under license in the United States by the Packard Motor Company, and by the summer of 1943, Packard Merlin-powered P-51s were coming off North American's assembly line. Merlin-powered P-51s, equipped with jettisonable drop tanks, had an operational range of more than 1,600 miles (2,500 km), and they mounted their first long-range bomber escort missions over Germany in mid-December 1943.

The Merlin engine was a liquid-cooled V-12 engine that was much lighter and more powerful than the Allison, and it had a two-stage supercharger, which allowed it to maintain its power at high altitudes. The Merlin engine greatly increased the Mustang's range and performance. With the Merlin, the Mustang could reach a top speed of over 440 mph, making it one of the fastest fighters of its time. The vastly increased range allowed it to escort bombers deep into enemy territory and engage in long-range dogfights without the need for refueling. Overall, the Merlin engine greatly enhanced the Mustang's capabilities and solidified its reputation as a top-performing fighter aircraft. Its combination of power, speed, and range made it a formidable opponent in the air and a crucial asset in the Allied victory during World War II.

General Dwight D. Eisenhower's Flight: On June 6, 1944, D-Day, General Dwight D. Eisenhower flew in a P-51 Mustang named "The Stars Look Down." This symbolic flight was intended to boost the morale of the Allied forces and symbolize the Allied commitment to the liberation of Europe.

P-51 Aces

Captain Don S. Gentile:

Don Gentile was a P-51 Mustang pilot with the 4th Fighter Group out of RAF Debden. He scored twenty-one confirmed aerial victories and became one of the leading American aces in the European theater. Gentile was known for his aggressive flying style and was awarded the Distinguished Service Cross. Sadly, he was killed in a T-33 crash on January 23rd, 1951.

Major George E. Preddy:

George Preddy was a P-51 Mustang pilot with the 352nd Fighter Group from RAF Bodney, Norfolk (nicknamed 'The Blue Nosed Bastards') He scored twenty-six confirmed aerial victories during the war and was known for his exceptional marksmanship. Preddy tragically lost his life in a friendly fire incident in December 1944.

Lieutenant Colonel John C. Meyer:

John Meyer, a P-51 Mustang pilot with the 487th Fighter Squadron at RAF Bodney, Norfolk, scored twenty-four aerial victories during the war. He later became a prominent figure in the U.S. Air Force and served as a commander in the Korean War.

19. 352nd Fighter Group Memorial, Bodney Camp, Norfolk (author).

Other P-51 Operators

Although the P-51 Mustang was primarily used by the USAAF during World War II, it was also used by several other allied nations. These nations include the United Kingdom, Australia, Canada, China, France, the Netherlands, and the Soviet Union.

United Kingdom: The UK mainly used the P-51 for long-range escort missions, as the aircraft's range and firepower made it well-suited for this role. The

P-51B and P-51C models were the most widely used by the RAF, with over 1,500 aircraft being delivered through the Lend-Lease program. The British also used the P-51 for ground attack and reconnaissance missions.

Australia also received P-51 Mustangs through the Lend-Lease program and used them primarily for reconnaissance and ground attack missions in the Pacific theater. The RAAF operated the P-51D and P-51K models, with some aircraft being modified for long-range maritime patrol.

Canada also received P-51 Mustangs through the Lend-Lease program, and they were mainly used for training purposes. However, a small number of Canadian-built P-51s were used for reconnaissance and ground attack missions in the European theater.

China received a large number of P-51s through the Lend-Lease program, and they were used primarily for ground attack and close air support missions against Japanese forces in China and Burma. The Chinese Air Force operated various models of the P-51, including the P-51B, P-51C, P-51D, and P-51K.

France also received P-51 Mustangs through the Lend-Lease program, and they were used by the Free French Air Force for reconnaissance and ground attack missions in Europe. Some French squadrons also operated the P-51 as a fighter-bomber.

Netherlands received P-51 Mustangs through the Lend-Lease program, and they were used by the Royal Netherlands East Indies Army Air Force for reconnaissance and ground attack missions in the Pacific theater.

Soviet Union received a small number of P-51 Mustangs through the Lend-Lease program, and they were used for reconnaissance and ground attack missions on the Eastern Front. The Soviet Union designated the P-51 as the F-6 and used it until the end of the war.

In conclusion, the P-51 Mustang was a vital asset to the VIII Fighter Wing, the 3rd AD, and other Allied units during World War II. Its speed, maneuverability, and long-range made it an excellent escort fighter. Its impact on the war efforts cannot be overstated, and it remains a symbol of American ingenuity (married with some British engine know-how!) during one of the most significant conflicts in history.

Chapter 9
Valor in the Skies: The 3rd Air Division's Standout Bombing Missions

The 3rd AD played a huge role in many key missions during World War II and some particularly notable missions and operations are detailed below.

The Schweinfurt Raids: A Trial by Fire

As dawn broke on October 14, 1943, the airfields scattered across England buzzed with activity, unprecedented even at the already intense pace of the Second World War. The USAAF was poised for a mission that would etch the name Schweinfurt into the annals of aerial warfare history forever.

The target was the industrial heart of Nazi Germany's ball bearing production, located in the

Bavarian city of Schweinfurt. This mission, later to be known as "Black Thursday," was a significant moment in the air campaign over Europe, testing the resolve, strategy, and mettle of the Allied aircrews and their commanders. This was the second time the targets were to be attacked, as there had been prior raid on August 17th, 1943.

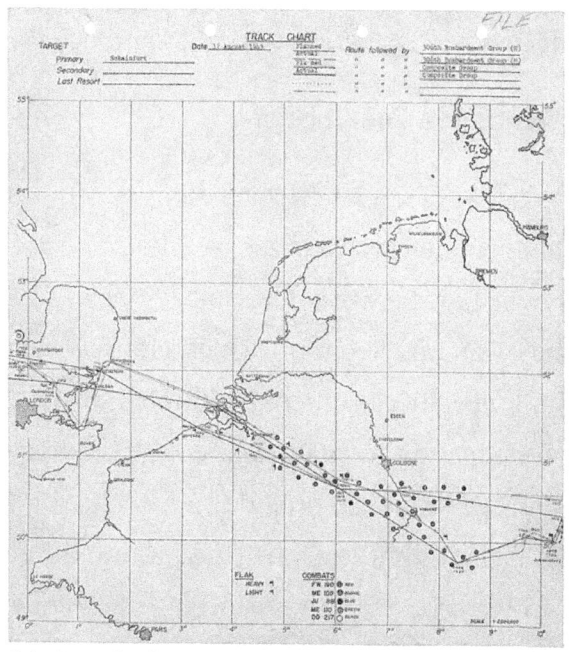

20. Track chart of the Schweinfurt–Regensburg mission, 17 August 1943.

The Target: Schweinfurt's Significance

Schweinfurt's factories were critical to the Nazi war machine, producing a significant portion of the ball bearings essential for aircraft, tanks, and vehicles. The USAAF had identified the crippling of ball bearing production as a strategic blow that could significantly impact Germany's ability to sustain its military efforts. Previous raids in August had shown the potential for severe disruption but at a high cost, prompting a reevaluation of tactics and objectives.

The Weather: A Foe Unseen

The mission faced its first challenge even before reaching enemy airspace: the weather. The autumn skies over Europe were notoriously fickle, and October 14 was no exception. Thick cloud cover, fog, and poor visibility plagued the bombers from take-off, complicating formation assembly and navigation. The weather also provided a measure of cover from German fighters, but it was a double-edged sword, obscuring targets and forcing the bombers to fly lower, within easier reach of anti-aircraft fire.

The Squadrons Involved

The mission comprised over 290 B-17 Flying Fortresses, divided among several bomb groups, including the 1st and 3rd AD's of the Eighth Air Force. These units included seasoned squadrons like the 100th, 95th and 91st Bomb Groups, all decorated for their precision and bravery under fire. Each group formed a crucial part of the intricate ballet that was a bombing raid, with tight formations designed to maximize defensive firepower against enemy attacks.

Key Personnel: Leadership in the Sky

Leadership in such perilous endeavors was paramount. Men like Brigadier General Frederick Castle, commanding the 4th Bombardment Wing, and Colonel Curtis LeMay, who devised the combat box formation to improve defensive capabilities, were instrumental. These leaders navigated not only their aircraft, but also the fine line between aggressive strategy and the preservation of their men. Pilots, navigators, bombardiers, and gunners, many of whom were in their early twenties, displayed courage and determination in the face of overwhelming odds. Names like Lieutenant Colonel Robert Rosenthal of the 100th Bomb Group, who led his squadron through ferocious fire to deliver their payload, became legends.

The Casualty Rate: A Grim Toll

The cost of the mission was staggering. Of the aircraft that took off, sixty B-17s were lost to enemy fire and another seventeen damaged beyond repair, resulting in a casualty rate of over 26%. The human cost was more harrowing, with approximately 600 airmen lost or captured. The crews faced relentless attacks from Luftwaffe fighters and flak batteries, testing the limits of their training and endurance. The loss of life and aircraft on this day underscored the brutal reality of the strategic bombing campaign over Europe.

Mission Success: A Pyrrhic Victory

The raid inflicted significant damage on Schweinfurt's ball-bearing plants, disrupting production and proving the strategic bombing concept. However, the high losses prompted a reevaluation of daylight bombing raids without adequate fighter escort. It wasn't until the introduction of long-range escort fighters like the P-51 Mustang that the USAAF could resume deep penetration raids into Germany with a measure of safety and effectiveness.

The Schweinfurt raids highlighted the complexities of aerial warfare and strategic bombing. The mission's mixed outcomes contributed to evolving tactics, including tighter formations and the importance of fighter escorts, shaping the future of the air war over Europe. The bravery and sacrifice of the airmen involved left an indelible mark on military history, serving as a testament to the determination and resilience of the Allied forces.

Reflection

"Black Thursday" remains a poignant chapter in the narrative of World War II, embodying the courage, innovation, and perseverance of the Allied aircrews. The lessons learned from the Schweinfurt raids informed subsequent operations, paving the way for the eventual Allied victory in Europe. The story of Schweinfurt is not just one of military strategy and conflict but a human story of bravery, sacrifice, and the relentless pursuit of victory.

Striking the Heart of the Third Reich

The 3rd AD's raids against the heart of the Third Reich were not merely assaults on physical structures, but strikes at the psychological core of Nazi power. Targeting the Reich's Capital Berlin, with its dense concentration of military, industrial, and governmental infrastructures, represented the apex of strategic targets within Nazi Germany. The city's defenses were formidable, protected by layers of anti-aircraft artillery (flak) and patrolled by seasoned Luftwaffe fighter pilots. For the 3rd AD, the challenge was not just to penetrate these defenses but to do so repeatedly, delivering their payloads with precision under the most adverse conditions.

Battling the Elements and the Enemy

Weather over Europe posed a significant challenge to bombing operations, and the Berlin raids were no exception. Crews often faced dense cloud cover, icing conditions, and unpredictable winds that complicated navigation and formation flying. These meteorological challenges were compounded by the ever-present threat of enemy interception. Despite these obstacles, the determination of the 3rd AD to reach and strike its targets remained unwavering.

Squadrons at the Vanguard, 3rd AD, equipped with B-17 Flying Fortresses, fielded several key squadrons in the raids on Berlin. Units such as the 94th, 95th, and 100th BGs were instrumental in these operations. Each group had honed their skills in the unforgiving skies over occupied Europe. Their participation in the Berlin raids was marked by tight formation flying, a tactic that maximized defensive firepower and offered some protection against enemy fighters.

Leadership in the Skies

Leadership within the 3rd AD was characterized by both strategic vision and personal bravery. Senior officers and squadron leaders alike understood the risks involved in the Berlin missions. Commanders such as Major General Curtis E. LeMay and Brigadier General Frederick W. Castle were instrumental in planning and executing these raids, often joining the crews in the air. Their leadership extended beyond tactics and strategy; they inspired their men to undertake missions that tested the limits of endurance and courage.

The Toll of War

The casualty rates during the Berlin raids reflected the high stakes of the campaign. The 3rd AD, like other units participating in these missions, suffered significant losses. Aircraft were lost to flak, mechanical failures, and enemy fighters. Each mission saw brave airmen sadly taken prisoner or killed in action. Despite these losses, the resolve of the division to fulfill its mission objectives never faltered.

Mission Success

Strategic Impact Assessing the success of the Berlin raids involves more than tallying destroyed targets or lost aircraft. These missions degraded the German war effort, disrupting transportation networks and damaging industrial facilities. Moreover, they forced the Luftwaffe to defend the capital, thus diluting its strength on other fronts. The psychological impact on the German military and civilian population, though difficult to quantify, was significant. The 3rd AD's role in these operations exemplified the strategic bombing doctrine's application. By targeting Berlin, hence the 'will' of the German people, the division contributed to the cumulative pressure on Nazi Germany, hastening its eventual collapse. The courage and sacrifice of the men involved left a permanent mark on the history of aerial warfare.

Reflections on Courage and Strategy

The Berlin raids undertaken by the 3rd AD were a confluence of strategic insight, technological capability, and human courage. The division's aircrews, navigating through hostile skies, delivered their deadly cargoes with precision, facing down both the natural elements and a determined enemy. The leadership, from the planners to the pilots, displayed a combination of tactical acumen and sheer resolve. The story of the 3rd AD in the Berlin raids is a poignant chapter in the broader narrative of World War II. It highlights the complexities of the air war over Europe and the indomitable spirit of those who fought it. Through their efforts, the Allied forces moved closer to victory, sustained by their belief in their cause and the bonds of brotherhood forged in the skies above Nazi Germany. The legacy of the 3rd AD, marked by both its achievements and its sacrifices, remains a powerful reminder of the cost of freedom and the valor required to secure it

Striking the Lifeblood of the Reich

The strategic bombing campaign against Nazi Germany reached a critical juncture with the initiation of the Oil Plan, targeting the lifeblood of the Wehrmacht's war machine: its oil refineries and production facilities. Within this campaign, the 3rd AD of the USAAF played a pivotal role, demonstrating the strategic acumen and operational bravery that characterized the Allied air effort. This chapter delves into the division's contribution to the oil raids, shedding light on the tactical intricacies, the human element, and the overall impact of these missions on the course of the Second World War.

The Strategic Imperative

The Allied command recognized that crippling the Nazi war effort required more than just bombing military targets and industrial complexes; it necessitated cutting off the fuel that powered the German military. By mid-1944, the focus sharply turned to oil refineries and synthetic oil plants across the Reich and occupied territories, and led to some of the 3rd AD's most challenging missions of the war. In 1925, Germany had developed the Fisher Tropes process to convert coal into synthetic fuel in a bid to combat their dependence on imports, and rumors of oil reserves running out elsewhere in the world. It was this process that allowed the German military to continue operating while oil supplies from other nations were scuttled by the Allied forces.

The Weather: An Ever-Present Adversary

The European weather continued to be a formidable opponent, with fog, rain, and cloud cover frequently complicating bombing missions. Navigating over long distances, often deep into enemy territory, the bombers of the 3rd AD had to contend with these meteorological challenges while maintaining formation integrity and avoiding detection for as long as possible. The unpredictability of the weather also meant that targets might be obscured at the last moment, requiring split-second decisions to proceed or abort the mission.

Squadrons on the Front Line

The 94th, 95th, and 100th BGs were at the forefront of the oil campaign and became synonymous with the oil raids, each participating in numerous sorties against refineries in places such as Merseburg, Leipzig, and Ploiești. These squadrons flew in tight formations, bristling with defensive armaments, to deliver their payloads with the best precision available at the time.

Leadership Amidst Adversity

The success of the oil raids hinged not just on strategy and technology but also on the leadership and courage of key personnel. Men like Major General William E. Kepner, commanding the 3rd AD, played a crucial role in planning and executing these raids. Squadron leaders and crew members, many of whom had flown multiple combat missions, demonstrated exceptional bravery and skill. Pilots, navigators, bombardiers, and gunners worked in concert to navigate the perilous skies, evade enemy defenses, and strike their targets with deadly accuracy. Pilots in the 3rd AD, flying their heavy bombers, were tasked with delivering precise strikes on critical oil production facilities deep within enemy territory. These missions were fraught with danger, requiring pilots to navigate through anti-aircraft fire, enemy fighters, and the challenging weather conditions to reach their targets.

Notable bomber pilots were individuals like Lt. Col. Addison Baker and Maj. John Jerstad of the 93rd BG who led the mission to Romania who posthumously received the Medal of Honor for their actions during the low-level bombing raid on the oil refineries at Ploiești, Romania, on August 1, 1943.

Collaboration Between Bombers and Fighters

The success of the oil raids was heavily dependent on the collaboration between the bomber crews of the 3rd AD and the fighter pilots from the 66th Fighter Wing. The bombers' ability to reach their targets and return home was significantly enhanced by the presence of these fighter escorts, who engaged German fighters and prevented them from disrupting the bombers' formations.

Casualties and Valor

The casualty rates among both bomber and fighter groups were high, reflecting the dangerous nature of their missions. Many were decorated for their valor with awards such as the Distinguished Flying Cross and the Silver Star, recognizing their courage and contribution to the Allied war effort.

Legacy of the Pilots

The pilots of the 3rd AD and the 66th Fighter Wing played a critical role in the success of the Allied strategic bombing campaign, particularly in the crippling of the Nazi oil production capabilities. Their actions not only demonstrated the importance of air superiority and precision bombing in modern warfare but also highlighted the human element of bravery, sacrifice, and skill in the face of daunting odds. The stories of the bomber pilots tasked with delivering their payloads under dire circumstances, and the fighter pilots who protected them, remain a testament to the collaborative effort required to achieve strategic objectives.

The Toll of the Campaign

The oil raids were among the most fiercely contested operations of the air war, with the Luftwaffe and German anti-aircraft defenses inflicting heavy casualties on the attacking bombers. The 3rd AD bore a significant share of these losses. Missions to heavily defended targets like the synthetic oil plants at Merseburg resulted in the heavy loss of numerous aircraft and crewmen. The Ploiești raid destroyed forty-two percent of the refining facility, striking a heavy blow to the Germans for several weeks. However, it took a heavy toll on the Allies, too. Fifty-four bombers were lost, and 532 of the 1,726 personnel involved died, were missing, or were taken prisoner.

Measuring Success

The impact of the oil raids on the German war effort was profound. By the autumn of 1944, the relentless bombing had significantly reduced Germany's oil production capacity, constraining the operations of the Wehrmacht and Luftwaffe. While the immediate aftermath of the raids often presented a mixed picture, with factories sometimes being repaired and production temporarily resumed, the long-term effect was undeniable: Germany was starved of the fuel essential for sustained military operations.

Reflections on Valor and Victory

The 3rd AD's participation in the oil campaign exemplifies the strategic shift in the Allied bombing effort from area bombing to precision strikes on critical infrastructure. This shift, while demanding more from the aircrews in terms of accuracy and exposure to danger, ultimately played a pivotal role in undermining the Nazi war machine.

The legacy of the 3rd AD in the oil campaign is not just one of strategic success but also of the human spirit's resilience in the face of overwhelming odds. It is a story of the relentless pursuit of a just cause: qualities that define the enduring nature of the 'Greatest Generation.'

Operation Argument: Big Week

As the bitter winter of 1944 gripped Europe, a pivotal moment in World War II unfolded with Operation Argument, colloquially known as "Big Week." This weeklong aerial onslaught, spanning from February 20 to 25, marked a turning point in the air war over

Europe. Among the primary actors in this dramatic operation were the 3 divisions of the Eighth Air Force, the RAF and the Fifteenth Air Force based in Italy. This section explores the 3rd AD's specific roles in Big Week and details the targets, weather conditions, squadrons involved, key personnel, casualty rates, and mission success.

Strategic Objectives

Operation Argument was conceived with a clear and ambitious strategic objective: to gain air superiority over the skies of Western Europe in preparation for the impending Allied invasion of Normandy (D-Day). To achieve this, the Allies aimed to deal a devastating blow to the Luftwaffe and disrupt Germany's aircraft production capabilities. The 3rd AD, particularly the B-17 Flying Fortresses, played a vital role in the fruition of this plan.

The Targets

Central to Big Week were the critical targets—aircraft factories, ball bearing plants, and transportation hubs—whose destruction would cripple the Luftwaffe's operational capacity and weaken Germany's ability to resupply its forces. The 3rd AD had specific targets within these categories, with the 4th, 13th, 45th, and 93rd Bombardment Wings tasked with pinpoint precision bombing.

Weather Challenges

The winter weather in Europe posed a formidable challenge. The skies were often overcast with dense cloud cover, which hindered visibility and increased the risk of collisions during formation flying. Additionally, freezing temperatures at high altitudes made for an arduous environment for both man and machine.

Units Involved

A combined force of 314 B-17s from the 94th, 95th, 96th, 100th, 385th, 388th, 390th, 447th, 452nd, and the 482nd BGs was dispatched to bomb the primary target of the German airfield at Tutow, Germany. Targets at Poznan and Kreising were the assigned primaries for the rest of the formation, although during the mission the formation leader decided the cloud cover over Poznan and Kreising would prevent bombing and so they reverted to bombing Rostock, Germnay, and other Targets of Opportunity (TOO). There was no fighter escort for this element.

105 aircraft attacked the German airfield at Tutow and surrounding areas; seventy-six aircraft bombed the aircraft industry at Rostock; and 155 aircraft bombed the remaining TOO. Six aircraft Failed to Return (FTR) - nineteen airmen were KIA, thirty taken as POW, and ten INT (Interned in Sweden). Thirty-seven aircraft were damaged. One battle-damaged aircraft was declared Damaged Beyond Repair (DBR) in a crash landing at Mutford, UK. [1]

Moments of Bravery

Operation Argument exemplified airmen of exceptional caliber.

In one memorable event on February 20, 1944, Pilot (Major) Alvah Chapman was attacked by a swarm of Luftwaffe Me-109's near the target. The aircraft lost its number three engine, the crankshaft broke, and the prop looked as though it would go flying off at any minute. A blade on the number four prop was torn off, and the throttle controls were ren-

---

1.

https://www.americanairmuseum.com/archive/mission/8th-air-force-226-big-week-day-1

dered useless. The brakes and flaps also suffered severe splintering. Two Me-109s moved in for the kill, thinking the Fortress was now a dead duck. In an effort to throw them off the trail, Capt. Delwyn Silver, copilot and deputy group leader, ordered the plane to spiral earthward in an attempt to mislead the Jerry fighters into believing the Fortress was crashing. The Germans clung to the pursuit and tailed the damaged giant in its flight downward, blazing away with everything they had for as long as they could. But miraculously, the B-17 and it's crew survived the attack and returned home successfully. Chapman later became the Commander of the 614th Bomb Squadron aged only 23. He flew a total of thirty-seven B-17 missions over Europe during the war and was awarded three Distinguished Flying Crosses and six Air Medals for acts of heroism and meritorious achievement while participating in aerial flight. Chapman retied from military service after the war and became the executive vice president and general manager of the *St. Petersburg Times*.

Another notable airman of the raid was Lt. Charles Betzel, who was a graduate of Davenport High School and was employed at the Iowa-Illinois Gas

& Electric Co. before entering the service in April 1942. Training as a bombardier, he received his wings and was commissioned as a 2nd Lieutenant in the Air Corps on May 8, 1943 at Victorville, California. Sent overseas, he was assigned as a bombardier in the 91st Bomb Group / 322nd Bomb Squadron. Betzel was shot down on February 20, 1944 on the homeward leg of his fifteenth mission, while flying as one of the 'Terrible Ten' in B-17F #42-29656 'Skunkface'. Two FW190 fighters attacked Skunkface and it crashed NNW of Mons, Belgium, although Betzel and some of his crewmen managed to bail out before impact. Betzel landed near a farm in Hainaut, Belgiu, with a broken ankle and minor head injuries. At first, he managed to evade German forces thanks to Belgian patriots and the COMETE evasion network (the Comet Line). However, he was later captured in a trap set by infiltrators who had organized a false evasion line and was ultimately held as a POW at Stalag Luft 3 and Stalag 7A in Moosburg, before being liberated by US forces in April 1945. Betzel survived the war and eventually died back home in the US in 1980.

Casualty Rate and Mission Success

Big Week exacted a heavy price. The casualty rate for the 3rd AD, as with the other divisions involved, was significant. The relentless barrage of flak and determined enemy fighter attacks took a toll on the men and machines. The sacrifices were felt deeply, and the loss of fellow airmen weighed heavily on the crews. Despite the adversity faced, Operation Argument was a resounding success. The combined efforts of the 3rd AD, along with other USAAF and RAF units, struck a crippling blow to the Luftwaffe and inflicted substantial damage on Germany's aircraft production infrastructure. Furthermore, the Allies achieved air superiority and paved the way for the successful D-Day landings.

D-Day, June 6, 1944

June 6, 1944, marked a day of destiny for the Allied forces. The largest amphibious invasion in history, codenamed Operation Overlord, was underway. At the heart of this historic endeavor stood the 3rd AD, a key component of the USAAF. This chapter explores the specific roles played by the bomb groups within the division during D-Day. From the targets and challenging weather conditions to the squadrons involved, key personnel, casualty rates, and mission success, we delve into the pivotal contributions of the 3rd AD on that fateful day.

The Strategic Objective

Operation Overlord aimed to establish a beachhead in Normandy, France, to launch the liberation of Western Europe from Nazi occupation. The 3rd AD's mission was to provide aerial support, bombard key targets, and create a path for the amphibious assault on the beaches of Normandy. The targets for the 3rd AD on D-Day were primarily German coastal defenses, artillery positions, and transportation infrastructure. Precision bombing was essential to weakening the enemy's ability to mount an effective defense against the approaching Allied forces. In the afternoon, road junctions at Coutances, Falaise, Lisieux, Saint-Lo, Thery-Harcourt, Vire, and Conde-Sur-Noiruea were targeted in Mission 395.

Weather Challenges

Weather prevented accurate targeting on the day, with clouds obscuring the targets; subsequently, most of the bombs fell 1,000 yards to the rear of the coastal defenses, as German survivors reported after the war.

Units Involved

The 3rd AD consisted of four BGs, each with its own squadrons. On D-Day, all the bomb groups of the 3rd AD were utilized, with a combined Eighth Air Force bomber force of 2,512 bombers launched.

Key Personnel

Division Commander: Major General Robert B. Williams was the overall commander for the 3rd AD during Operation Overlord. The "First Force", led by Col. Luper with Lt. Charles D. Brannan as pilot, began taking off at 0430 hours, followed by the "Third Force", at 0450 hours, led by Major Fred A. Spencer with Captain Russell M. Selwyn as pilot. The formation assembly was finalized as dawn broke, and the English Coast was crossed at 0632 hours. At mid-channel, the cloud cover was ten-tenths. Yet looking out in front through a hole in the clouds and under the overcast, one could see some of the thousands of watercraft on their way to the invasion.

Casualty Rate and Mission Success

D-Day was a day of immense sacrifice for land and naval forces, but the poor weather had also prevented the Luftwaffe from getting airborne and providing any credible threat. Consequently, very few Allied bombers were lost. The "First Force" dropped its bombs at 0700 hours. The "Third Force" dropped at 0710 hours. At the same time, the primary targets were being shelled by warships and hit by dive bombers. The whole invasion coast was obscured by clouds, and it was not until the formation approached the English coast that the many invasion craft could be seen again. No enemy fighters or flak were encountered. All planes returned to the base, and crews stood by for a second mission, but none was ordered. The bombing of enemy defenses and infrastructure played a significant role in weakening the German positions along the coast, facilitating the safe landing of Allied troops on the Normandy beaches.

Mission Success

The success of the 3rd Air Division's missions on D-Day can be measured by the fact the Allied forces successfully established a beachhead in Normandy. Despite the adverse weather, the division's bombing runs aided in securing key objectives along the coast, allowing the infantry to advance and ultimately achieve a foothold in France. D-Day marked the beginning of the liberation of Western Europe and the eventual defeat of Nazi Germany. The 3rd AD's contributions on that historic day epitomized the bravery, skill, and dedication of the airmen who played a vital role in the liberation of France and the eventual end of World War II in Europe.

Chapter 10
Guardians of the Skies: The 3rd Air Division's Aces

In the vast theater of World War II, where every act of valor contributed to the tapestry of Allied victory, the USAAF 3rd AD also carved its name into the history books with their incredible strokes of bravery and strategic brilliance. As part of the mighty Eighth Air Force, the 3rd AD was a critical force in the strategic bombing campaign over Europe, targeting Nazi war machinery with relentless precision. This chapter aims to shine a light on the key individual airmen of the 3rd AD, whose extraordinary feats not only defined the success of their missions but also the very essence of aerial warfare during the conflict.

Operating from bases in England, the division's B-17 Flying Fortresses and B-24 Liberators became symbols of hope and liberation across the war-torn skies of Europe. Behind the throttles, highly secretive bomb sights, and machine guns of these formidable aircraft, were men of unparalleled courage and determination—pilots, navigators, bombardiers, gunners, and crew chiefs—whose stories of heroism resonate with the spirit of sacrifice and duty.

Among these notable airmen was Brigadier General Frederick W. Castle, a commanding officer whose leadership and valor on a fateful mission over Germany earned him the Medal of Honor posthumously. When his B-17 was critically damaged by enemy fighters, Castle maintained control, ensuring his crew could bail out, tragically sacrificing his own life for theirs. His actions embody the division's ethos of leadership and sacrifice.

Another figure of renown was Lieutenant Colonel Robert Rosenthal, a pilot who flew an astonishing fifty-two missions with the 100th Bomb Group, the "Bloody Hundredth." Rosenthal's aircraft, "Rosie's Riveters," became a beacon of resilience, surviving numerous battles and returning its crew safely against overwhelming odds. His leadership and bravery under fire earned him multiple decorations, including the Distinguished Service Cross.

Captain John "Lucky" Luckadoo, a co-pilot and pilot within the division, narrowly escaped death on multiple occasions, completing twenty-five missions at a time when the life expectancy for bomber crews was brutally short. Luckadoo's experiences provide a vivid account of the dangers faced by airmen, highlighting the precarious line between life and death in the skies over Europe.

These airmen, along with countless others, were the vanguard of the Allied strategic bombing offensive, tasked with dismantling the Nazi war machine piece by piece. Their missions were fraught with peril—flak-filled skies, enemy fighters, and the ever-present threat of mechanical failure—yet they pressed on, driven by a sense of duty and a commitment to freedom.

This chapter explores the lives of these remarkable individuals and many more, drawing from mission reports, personal diaries, and historical analyses to paint a portrait of valor, resilience, and innovation. Through their stories, we explore the strategic significance of the 3rd AD's campaigns, the evolution of air warfare tactics, and the personal cost of aerial combat.

We must never forget the nameless individuals who manned the bases back home who are often forgotten about in tales of war; the glory is normally held by the 'Aces', but without their base support staffs, the Aces would not have their legacies! This chapter is therefore also dedicated to the thousands of unsung heroes of the USAAF who fed, maintained, administered, and cared for the brave airmen of the 3rd!

As we journey through the narratives of these key airmen, we learn they were not just guardians of the skies, but architects of peace whose contributions helped shape the course of history.

Lieutenant General Curtis LeMay

21. Lieutenant General Curtis E. LeMay, USAF

Lieutenant General Curtis E. LeMay is one of the most prominent and influential military leaders in American history, particularly noted for his roles during World War II and the Cold War. While he is perhaps most famously associated with his leadership in the strategic bombing campaigns against Japan and later roles, including heading the Strategic Air Command (SAC) and serving as the Air Force Chief of Staff, LeMay did indeed play a significant role in the European Theater of Operations as well.

Early Career and World War II

Curtis LeMay was born in Columbus, Ohio, in 1906. He graduated from the United States Army Air Corps Flying School in 1932 and rose through the ranks in the interwar years. By the time the United States entered World War II, LeMay was a colonel and quickly became known for his expertise in navigation, bombing strategy, and air tactics.

Role in the 3rd Air Division

During World War II, LeMay initially served in the European Theatre, where he was instrumental in developing effective bombing strategies for the USAAF. His involvement with the 3rd AD came as part of this broader role. Among his contributions to aerial warfare, the "7-minute bombing run" strategy stands out as a pivotal tactic designed to enhance the effectiveness of bombing missions while minimizing the exposure of aircraft to enemy defenses.

Background and Development

LeMay's approach to strategic bombing evolved through his experiences in both the European and Pacific theaters. Recognizing the high risks faced by bomber crews due to prolonged exposure to enemy anti-aircraft artillery (AAA) and fighter intercepts, LeMay sought ways to reduce the time bombers spent over target areas while improving accuracy. He analyzed previous mission data and realized the extant tactics of jinking the aircraft to avoid flak and conducting short bombing runs meant that more than fifty percent of bombs dropped were falling wide of their targets.

The '7-Minute Bombing Run'

The "7-minute bombing run" strategy was a direct outcome of LeMay's emphasis on precision and efficiency. The tactic involved a tight, disciplined approach to the bombing process, from the initial point (IP) to the bomb release.

<u>Formation Tightening</u>: As the bomber formation approached the IP i.e. the lead-up to the target area, crews would tighten their formation to improve mutual defense and bombing accuracy.

<u>Rapid and Precise Navigation</u>: Navigators and pilots worked in concert to ensure the most direct and accurate approach to the target, minimizing deviations and the time spent in enemy airspace.

Streamlined Bombing Process: The bomb run, from IP to the release point, was executed with precision timing, with crews trained to complete the process within a span of approximately seven minutes. This minimized the window during which the formation was most vulnerable to AAA and fighter attacks.

Quick Egress: After bomb release, formations would rapidly exit the target area, employing evasive maneuvers as needed to reduce the risk of being hit by flak or intercepted by enemy fighters.

Impact and Effectiveness

LeMay's 7-minute bombing run strategy significantly impacted the USAAF's bombing campaigns by improving mission success rates and reducing casualties among the bomber crews. This approach required rigorous training and discipline, as each crew member's actions needed to be precisely coordinated with the rest of the formation.

Strategic Bombing in the Pacific

LeMay further adapted his tactics when he took command of B-29 Superfortress operations against Japan in the Pacific Theater. He implemented low-altitude night bombing using incendiary bombs, a strategy that, while controversial, was credited with crippling Japan's industrial capacity. Though different from the high-altitude precision bombing runs over Europe, this tactic also reflected LeMay's pragmatic approach to achieving strategic objectives.

Leadership and Tactics

LeMay was recognized for his no-nonsense leadership style and his insistence on precision and discipline. He demanded a lot from his crews but was also deeply committed to reducing the loss of life among his men and improving the effectiveness of bombing missions. His strategies, while sometimes controversial for their ruthlessness, were credited with significantly degrading the industrial capacity of Nazi Germany and later the Japanese Empire.

Post-World War II

After his service in Europe, LeMay was transferred to the China-Burma-India theater and later to the Pacific theater, where he led the firebombing of Tokyo. Following the war, LeMay's career continued to ascend. He played a critical role in organizing the

Berlin Airlift (1948-1949), led the SAC during much of the Cold War, and served as the Air Force Chief of Staff from 1961 to 1965. LeMay was also a vice presidential candidate in the 1968 U.S. presidential election. Lieutenant General Curtis E. LeMay's legacy is complex, marked by his innovative tactics and leadership that significantly impacted air warfare strategy and the outcome of World War II, as well as his influential post-war military career. He died on October 1, 1990, in a hospital at March Air Force Base, California.

Legacy

Curtis LeMay's innovations in bombing strategy, including the 7-minute bombing run, underscore his legacy as a strategist who significantly advanced aerial warfare's effectiveness. His tactics have been studied and adapted in various forms in military academies and strategic studies, highlighting his enduring impact on military doctrine.

Brigadier General Frederick Walker Castle

Brigadier General Frederick Walker Castle (October 14, 1908 – December 24, 1944) was a senior officer in the USAAF during World War II and a posthumous recipient of the Medal of Honor—the highest military decoration awarded by the United States government.

Early Life and Military Career

Frederick W. Castle was born in Manila, Philippines, where his father was stationed as an officer in the United States Army. He grew up with a strong military influence and pursued a military career, graduating from the United States Military Academy at West Point in 1930. Initially commissioned in the Corps of Engineers, Castle transferred to the Air Corps in 1931 where he began a career that would lead him into the highest echelons of the Army Air Forces.

World War II Service

With the United States' entry into World War II, Castle quickly rose through the ranks, reflecting his abilities and the urgent need for experienced leadership in the rapidly expanding air force. He served in various staff positions before taking on more direct command roles in the strategic bombing campaign against Nazi Germany. Castle was assigned to the Eighth Air Force, which was responsible for the daylight strategic bombing campaign over occupied Europe and Germany. His leadership skills were put to the test as he helped plan and execute numerous bombing missions that targeted critical industrial and military infrastructure.

The Medal of Honor Mission

On December 24, 1944, during the Battle of the Bulge, Brigadier General Castle was serving as the air commander of a large formation of B-17 bombers from the 487th Bomb Group out of RAF Lavenham, England, on a mission to attack enemy airfields in support of the ground forces engaged in the battle. His aircraft was severely damaged by German anti-aircraft fire shortly after crossing into enemy territory. Despite the damage, Castle refused to turn back or seek cover, knowing the importance of the mission to the overall battle effort. With his plane on fire and losing altitude, he ordered his crew to bail out. Castle remained at the controls to ensure his crew could escape, sacrificing his own life in the process. His plane eventually crashed near Hods, Belgium, and he was killed.

Legacy and Honors

For his "conspicuous gallantry in action and intrepidity at the risk of his life above and beyond the call of duty," Castle was posthumously awarded the Medal of Honor. His leadership and selflessness exemplify the highest ideals of military service and sacrifice. Frederick W. Castle's memory is honored in various ways, including the naming of Castle Air Force Base in California (closed in 1995) and the establishment of a memorial at the crash site in Belgium. He is buried in the Henri-Chapelle American Cemetery and Memorial in Belgium, resting among the soldiers he led and served. Brigadier General Castle's story is a poignant reminder of the bravery and leadership of the United States Army Air Forces' officers during World War II. His actions and sacrifice are emblematic of the countless others who served and sacrificed in the skies over Europe to ensure victory and secure peace.

Colonel Robert Kelly

Colonel Robert H. Kelly sadly has one of the shortest careers as a commanding officer in the history of the 3rd AD. He was the Commanding Officer of the 100th Bomb Group based at RAF Thorpe Abbotts from April 19 to April 28, 1944. He was killed in action after 1 week and 2 days, over Sottevast on a bombing mission on April 28, 1944. Colonel Kelly was posthumously awarded the Distinguished Flying Cross, Legion of Merit, and the Order of the Purple Heart, which brought pride and consolation to his wife, Mrs. Lols C. Kelly, and their two young sons.

At take-off time on April 28, 1944, the new commander elected to bump the 100th's best flight leader (Captain Jack Swartout) and lead the mission himself. The results were a disaster; two aircraft were lost when the Colonel elected to make a second run over the target at the same altitude and on the same heading. Among the KIAs was Captain William Lakin who was on his last mission, and the 100th's beloved lead navigator, Captain Joseph "bubbles" Payne; said by Jim Brown and Harry Crosby to have been the best. Also shot down that day in B-17 'Noball' were:

- Lieutenant Maurice Cain - Bombardier - POW

- Lieutenant Herbert Alf - Command Pilot - POW

- Technical Sergeant Leo Cannon - Radio operator/Gunner - POW

- Technical Sergeant James Brown - Top Turret Engineer - KIA

- Staff Sergeant Albert Freitas - Ball Turret Gunner - POW

- Staff Sergeant John Spiker - Waist Gunner- KIA

- Staff Sergeant Joseph Richard - Waist Gunner - POW

- Staff Sergeant Delbert Barnhart - Tail Gunner – KIA

Joseph "Bubbles" Payne, Technical Sergeant James C. Brown and Staff Sergeant Albert M. Freitas were all members of the original air echelon. With the exception of Magee Fuller, they were the last of the "Original 100th" to become casualties. Technical Sergeant Cannon joined the group in August 1943 after his original crew (F.H. Meadows) was shot down at Bremen October 8, 1943. Captain William G. Lakin had been with the group prior to October 1 943.

Lieutenant Colonel Robert Rosenthal

Lieutenant Colonel Robert Rosenthal was an iconic figure in the USAAF during World War II, serving with distinction as a bomber pilot in the 100th Bomb Group, famously known as the "Bloody Hundredth." His remarkable story of courage, leadership, and survival amidst some of the most dangerous bombing missions over Nazi-occupied Europe exemplifies the valor and resilience of the airmen of the Eighth Air Force.

22. Lieutenant Colonel
Robert Rosenthal

Early Life and Military Career

Robert Rosenthal was born in Brooklyn, New York, in 1917. He graduated from Brooklyn Law School and was practicing law when the United States entered World War II. He enlisted in the USAAF, motivated by a strong sense of duty and a desire to fight against the tyranny of the Nazi regime, and was posted to join the 100th stationed in England.

Acts of Valor

Throughout his service, Rosenthal displayed extraordinary bravery and skill. He flew a total of fifty-two combat missions, a remarkable feat given the high casualty rates among bomber crews. Rosenthal's aircraft were often heavily damaged by enemy fire, but his adept piloting and leadership ensured the survival and success of his crew on numerous occasions. One of Rosenthal's most notable missions was the raid on Munster on October 10, 1943, one of the bloodiest days for the 100th Bomb Group when they suffered significant losses. Despite intense enemy fire and damage to his aircraft, Rosenthal managed to complete the mission and eventually return safely to England, a credit to his piloting prowess and determination.

Awards and Recognition

For his gallantry in action, Rosenthal was awarded several high honors, including the Distinguished Service Cross, the Silver Star with three oak leaf clusters, the Distinguished Flying Cross with five oak leaf clusters, and the Air Medal with seven oak leaf clusters. These decorations reflect his exceptional service and the high regard in which he was held by his peers and commanders.

Post-War Life and Legacy

After the war, Robert Rosenthal continued to serve in the military before returning to civilian life. He resumed his law career and also participated in the prosecution of Nazi war criminals during the Nuremberg Trials, further contributing to the cause of justice he had fought for during the war. Rosenthal's legacy is one of heroism and leadership under the most challenging conditions. His life and military service continue to inspire those who learn of his contributions to one of history's most pivotal conflicts.

Lieutenant Colonel Addison Baker

The morning of August 1, 1943, dawned with a tense anticipation in the air. From Benghazi, Libya, aircrews prepared for one of the most audacious bombing raids of World War II. The target was the oil refineries at Ploiești, Romania, a vital artery in the Nazi war machine, providing the bulk of the petroleum fueling Hitler's forces. Among the men gearing up for the mission was Lieutenant Colonel Addison Baker, commanding officer of the 93 BG. Baker was no stranger to the dangers of aerial combat. With several missions under his belt, he had earned a reputation for his calm under pressure, unyielding leadership, and deep commitment to his crew and country. On this day, however, Baker and his co-pilot, Major John L. Jerstad, would face a challenge unlike any before.

The mission, codenamed "Operation Tidal Wave," was to fly at an exceptionally low altitude, evading radar detection, to deliver a crippling blow to the Axis oil production capabilities. As the morning sun crept over the horizon, Baker and Jerstad boarded their B-24 Liberator, nicknamed "Hell's Wench." The air was thick with the promise of the impending battle as the engines roared to life, a chorus of power and determination. Baker's gaze was fixed forward, his mind racing through the mission parameters, the route, and the potential anti-aircraft and fighter opposition they would face. The flight to Ploiești was fraught with tension. The formation flew incredibly low, skimming the treetops to maintain the element of surprise. Baker's leadership was paramount, keeping the formation tight and focused amidst the ever-present threat of discovery.

As they approached Ploiești, the air grew heavy with the smell of oil and the ominous clouds of smoke billowing from the refineries. It wasn't long before the flak began, a deadly rain of anti-aircraft fire filling the sky. Hell's Wench took a direct hit, its engines catching fire and the aircraft beginning to lose altitude rapidly. In that moment, Baker's resolve was tested as never before. The easy choice, the safe choice, would have been to turn back or order the crew to bail out. But Baker knew the mission's importance and the impact it could have on the war effort.

Turning to Jerstad, a silent agreement passed between them: they would see the mission through, no matter the cost. With the aircraft aflame and losing power, Baker maintained the formation lead, guiding his group towards the target. The refineries loomed ahead, a maze of pipes and tanks that were the lifeblood of the enemy's war effort. Through the smoke and fire, Baker and Jerstad made their bombing run, delivering their payload directly on target. As they turned to make their escape, there was no illusion of survival. Hell's Wench was beyond saving;

its fate was sealed. Yet, Baker's leadership and sacrifice had ensured the success of the mission.

His actions inspired his crew and the rest of the formation to press on, completing one of the most daring bombing raids of the war. Lieutenant Colonel Addison Baker and Major John L. Jerstad were posthumously awarded the Medal of Honor for their bravery, leadership, and sacrifice. Their actions on that fateful day in August demonstrated the highest ideals of courage and duty.

The raid on Ploiești would be remembered as one of the most challenging and costly missions of World War II, with a heavy toll paid in men and machines. Yet, the bravery of men like Addison Baker ensured the mission's objectives were met, dealing a significant blow to the Axis war effort.

As the sun set on the battle-scarred landscapes of Europe, the legacy of Addison Baker and his crew lived on, a beacon of hope and resilience in the darkest of times. Their story, a chapter in the broader narrative of the war, serves as a reminder of the cost of freedom and the price of victory.

Lieutenant Colonel Everett Blakely

Everett Ernest Blakely (July 1, 1919 – September 21, 2004) was a career officer of the United States Air Force. He was a highly decorated B-17 pilot with the "Bloody Hundredth" during the war. He received eleven medals for his service, including the Silver Star for "gallantry in action," the Distinguished Flying Cross for "heroism or extraordinary achievement during aerial flight", and the Air Medal with four oak leaf clusters.

His Beloved B-17, "Just a Snappin":

- Blakely primarily flew a B-17 named "Just a Snappin'", known for its resilience.

- The aircraft sustained significant damage on several occasions, including heavy flak and fighter attacks.

- Blakely and the crew of his plane "Just A Snappin'" long held the record for the most enemy aircraft shot down on a single mission, which was a phenomenal nine Luftwaffe aircraft during Mission 111, a feat that earned him the Distinguished Flying Cross and the Silver Star. The crew's record for the most number of shoot downs stood for decades.

- During Mission 111 on July 10th, 1943, which was Blakely's eighteenth mission, "Just a Snappin'" employed the first use of aluminum strips, which were dropped to jam German radar (what became known as "Chaff" or "Window").

- During this mission, "Just a Snappin'" took heavy fire and lost two engines causing it to lose altitude and nearly requiring her to ditch in the North Sea, tragically claiming the life of crew member Staff Sergeant Lester Saunders.

- Despite the heavy damage, Blakely managed to bring the plane back to England and crash-landed at an unused RAF base. Five crew other crew members were injured and received purple hearts.

- The salvage crew counted over 800 holes in

the B-17 from flak, machine gun bullets, and twenty millimeter cannon shells.

- Everett Blakely received his nation's third-highest medal for gallantry, the Silver Star, for his bravery that day.

- After the war, Blakely continued his service in the USAF for a total of twenty-seven years before retiring from service and starting a new career at Lockheed Air in Burbank, California. He retired from Lockheed in the late 1980s and died on September 21, 2004, aged 85 years old.

Capt John Luckadoo

Captain John "Lucky" Luckadoo served as a B-17 Flying Fortress co-pilot and pilot in the USAAF during World War II, specifically within the renowned 100th. Born in Chattanooga, Tennessee, in 1922, Luckadoo enlisted in the USAAF shortly after the United States entered World War II. His nickname, "Lucky," is a testament to his remarkable survival through twenty-five combat missions over Nazi-occupied Europe.

Awards and Recognition

During his service with the 100th at RAF Thorpe Abbotts, Luckadoo flew all twenty-five missions of his tour of duty and remained survive unscathed earned him his nickname and the admiration of his peers. For his service, Luckadoo received several commendations, including the Distinguished Flying Cross, awarded for heroism or extraordinary achievement while participating in aerial flight. He also earned the Air Medal with multiple oak leaf clusters, recognizing single acts of heroism or meritorious achievement while participating in aerial flight.

Post-War Life

After the war, Luckadoo continued to serve in the military for a time before transitioning to a successful civilian career. Despite the passage of years, he has remained an active voice in preserving the history and legacy of World War II airmen, sharing his experiences with new generations to ensure the sacrifices and contributions of his comrades are not forgotten. As of writing this book in February 2024, Luckadoo is still alive, aged 101 years old!

Legacy

Captain John "Lucky" Luckadoo's story is a powerful reminder of the courage and resilience of the young men who served in the bomber crews of World War II. His survival through twenty-five missions over some of the most heavily defended skies in Europe is a credit not only to his skill and luck but also to the spirit of determination that defined the Allied effort to defeat the Axis powers. Luckadoo's contributions, along with those of his fellow airmen, continue to be celebrated as part of the rich history of the USAAF and the broader narrative of World War II.

Master Sergeant Hewitt Dunn

Master Sergeant Hewitt T. 'Buck' Dunn is a remarkable figure in military history, renowned for his extraordinary service as a B-17 bomber crewman with the "Bloody Hundredth". Dunn survived **104 combat missions** performing the roles of gunner, flight engineer and radio operator over Nazi-occupied Europe, which is truly extraordinary.

Significance of 104 Combat Missions

Completing 104 combat missions in this context is a remarkable achievement. The average expectancy for bomber crews at various points in the war could be measured in just a handful of missions before being shot down or otherwise put out of action. Dunn's survival across so many sorties reflects not only his personal durability and dedication, but also the evolving tactics and technologies that helped protect Allied aircrews, such as improved formation flying, electronic countermeasures, and the deployment of long-range fighter escorts like the P-51 Mustang.

Legacy and Recognition

While specific details about each of Dunn's missions may not be widely documented, the overarching story of his service highlights the broader narrative of the thousands of aircrew members who risked, and often lost, their lives in the aerial campaign over Europe. Master Sergeant Dunn's story stands as a tribute to the courage and endurance of these airmen. After the war, veterans like Dunn carried with them the memories of their experiences, contributing to the legacy of the Greatest Generation through their stories and sacrifices.

Conclusion
Reflection and Impact

In the records of history, the 3rd AD of the USAAF during World War II stands as one of the greatest examples of the most extraordinary courage and steadfast dedication of its airmen. These brave men, flying giant, formidable aircraft like the B-17 Flying Fortress and the B-24 Liberator, faced the unimaginable danger in the skies of Europe to execute their missions with remarkable precision and valor.

As we've shown many times in this book, the 3rd AD's role in the aerial bombardment campaign over Europe was pivotal to the broader Allied strategy. Their missions aimed to weaken the Axis war machine, disrupt supply lines, and ultimately hasten the end of a devastating conflict. It was a strategy that adhered to the principles and tactics of its time, when the distinction between military and civilian targets was not as clear-cut as we understand it today. Heroic figures battled in the skies above Europe in both bomber and fighter aircraft alike, such that we enjoy democratic freedoms today. Brave men such as Master Sergeant Hewitt T. 'Buck' Dunn who flew 104 missions, when he could have gone home after twenty five; Lt Col Everett Ernest Blakely, whose aircraft shot down nine enemy fighters in one mission, a record for the war; George Preddy with his twenty six enemy kills launching from the grass airstrip of RAF Bodney, deep in the central rural belt of Norfolk. They fought bravely then for our freedoms today.

As we reflect upon these courageous aviators and their role in the war effort, it is essential to consider the ethical complexities that surround the celebration of aerial bombardment as a tactic. While the targeting principles of that era deemed certain civilian targets as legitimate, the passage of time has brought a greater understanding of the consequences and moral dilemmas associated with such actions.

The cost of civilian lives and the suffering inflicted upon innocent populations cannot be understated, nor can it be justified by the standards of today's ethical norms. The horrors of war, witnessed by those on the ground and those in the air, have left an unforgettable mark on history, and serve as a permanent reminder of the need for humanity and to strive for peace and reconciliation. After the war, the 1949 Geneva Conventions further outlawed the mass bombing of civilian populations for strategic effect and introduced targeting principles such as humanity, military necessity, proportionality and distinction.

While we honor the valor and sacrifices of the 3rd AD and countless others who served during World War II, we must also approach history with humility and a commitment to understanding the evolving ethics of warfare. Celebrating the bravery of these airmen should not overshadow the ethical complexities of their actions. Instead, it should remind us of the enduring human spirit in the face of adversity and challenge us to advocate for a world where diplomacy and peace prevail over the ravages of war.

In commemorating the legacy of the 3rd AD, we honor not only their courage but also our shared responsibility to learn from history's lessons and work towards a future where the horrors of aerial bombardment are relegated to the past, replaced by the pursuit of a more equitable and peaceful world.

About the Author

Daniel (Dan) L Couzens served in the British Armed Forces for 22 years, deploying across the world on military operations both as a British Army soldier and latterly as a Royal Air Force Officer. Dan was lucky enough to travel to all seven continents during his service, from the cold tundra's of the Falkland Islands to the warzones of Iraq, Afghanistan and Former Yugoslavia.

Dan was raised in Norfolk, surrounded by the derelict military buildings of former World War II airbases and the Stanford Army Training Area to the south. His childhood spent exploring these locations sparked a keen interest in aircraft and military affairs. Dan's Grandfather was a foreman for Walter E Lawrence Ltd, who was instrumental in helping airfield construction all over Norfolk and Suffolk. Dan spent his childhood listening to his grandfather's tales of the war, from building underground tunnels, to 'C' type hangars with huge doors filled with sand and shingle to stop blast fragmentation.

After leaving military service, Dan returned to Norfolk with his wife and two children. He now lives amongst the shadows of the valiant souls who launched their bombers and fighters from just around the corner, such that we all have the freedom and democracy we enjoy today.

We thank them for their service.

Picture Credits

Whilst all the pictures used in the book have been sourced as royalty free, credit is given below for numbered images.

1. https://commons.wikimedia.org/wiki/File:RAF_Bury_St_Edmunds_-_94th_Bombardment_Group_-_B-17_44-8158.jpg

2. https://commons.wikimedia.org/wiki/File:Rattlesden-07-may-1946.png

3. https://commons.wikimedia.org/wiki/File:RAF_Lavenham_-_Landing.jpg

4. https://commons.wikimedia.org/wiki/File:Former_RAF_Sudbury_from_the_air_-_geograph.org.uk_-_2404661.jpg

5. https://commons.wikimedia.org/wiki/File:Thorpeabbotsafld-13nov46.png

6. https://commons.wikimedia.org/wiki/File: RAF_Framlingham_-_Control_Tower.jpg

7. https://commons.wikimedia.org/wiki/File: RAF_Deopham_Green_-_452d_Bombardment_Group_B-17G_42-192622.jpg

8. Daniel L Couzens

9. https://commons.wikimedia.org/wiki/File: B-17F_%22Tom_Paine%22_of_the_388th_Bomb_Group,_WW2.jpg

10. https://commons.wikimedia.org/wiki/File: B-17G-70-BO_Fortress_Serial_43-37683_in_England,_WW2.jpg

11. https://commons.wikimedia.org/wiki/File: RAF_Great_Ashfield_-_31_March_1944_-_Airfield.jpg

12. https://commons.wikimedia.org/wiki/File: RAF_Eye_-_16_July_1943_-_Airphoto.jpg

13. https://commons.wikimedia.org/wiki/File: 493d_Bombardment_Group_B-17_Flying_Fortress_Formation.jpg

14. https://commons.wikimedia.org/wiki/File:B-17_FLYING_FORTRESS_3view.jpg

15. https://commons.wikimedia.org/wiki/File:B-24_LIBERATOR_3view.jpg

16. https://commons.wikimedia.org/wiki/File:55fg-Nuthampstead.jpg

17. https://commons.wikimedia.org/wiki/File:352fg-p47.jpg

18. https://commons.wikimedia.org/wiki/File:359th_Fighter_Group_-_P-51D_Mustangs.jpg

19. Daniel L Couzens

20. https://commons.wikimedia.org/wiki/File:Track_chart_of_the_Schweinfurt%E2%80%93Regensburg_mission,_17_August_1943.jpg

21. https://commons.wikimedia.org/wiki/File:Lt_Gen_Curtis_E._LeMay.jpg

22. https://en.wikipedia.org/wiki/Robert_Rosenthal_(USAAF_officer)

Printed in Great Britain
by Amazon